W9-BOM-362

SECOND EDITION

HOW TO BUY
FORECLOSED
REAL ESTATE
FOR A FRACTION
OF ITS VALUE

SECOND EDITION

HOW TO BUY
FORECLOSED
REAL ESTATE

FOR A FRACTION
OF ITS VALUE

Theodore J. Dallow

Adams Media Corporation
Avon, Massachusetts

Copyright ©2000, Theodore J. Dallow. All rights reserved.
This book, or parts thereof, may not be reproduced in any form without
permission from the publisher; exceptions are made for brief excerpts
used in published reviews.

Published by
Adams Media, an F+W Publications Company
57 Littlefield Street, Avon, MA 02322. U.S.A.
www.adamsmedia.com

ISBN: 1-58062-258-5

Printed in Canada.

J I H G F

Library of Congress Cataloging-in-Publication Data
Dallow, Theodore, J.
How to buy foreclosed real estate for a fraction of its value /
Theodore J. Dallow.—2nd ed.
p.   cm.
ISBN 1-58062-258-5
1. Real estate investment. 2. House buying. 3. Foreclosure. I. Title.
HD1382.5 .D35   2000
332.63'24--dc21   00-035593
CIP

This publication is designed to provide accurate and authoritative information with
regard to the subject matter covered. It is sold with the understanding that the publisher
is not engaged in rendering legal, accounting, or other professional advice. If legal
advice or other expert assistance is required, the services of a competent professional
person should be sought.
—From a *Declaration of Principles* jointly adopted by a Committee of the American
Bar Association and a Committee of Publishers and Associations

Cover photo ©Superstock by Roy King.

This book is available at quantity discounts for bulk purchases.
For information, call 1-800-872-5627.

To your future.

Contents

It may be a cliché to think of home ownership as the American Dream, but there is still truth to the notion.

What is a foreclosure? What is the difference between a mortgagor and a mortgagee? What are the five covenants of a mortgage? What are the root causes of a foreclosure proceeding?

Why must you know the bank's point of view? What are the stages of foreclosure? How can you tell if you're getting what you think you're getting? What research is involved in foreclosure purchases?

How do you find people whose properties are facing foreclosure? Who will you be dealing with? Should you consider lease arrangements? What are "due on sale" clauses?

Why do banks prefer to get rid of their owned real estate? What changes have taken place in recent years that have affected the way foreclosures are handled? How do you submit a bid? What about HUD and VA offerings?

When you can't sell and must get out, there's a way to
avoid the carrying expenses and/or foreclosure.

What are tax sales and sheriff's sales? How do they
differ from foreclosure sales? What are the major
nonmonetary reasons for default?

What are the three types of people who look to
purchase foreclosures? How should you handle
financing? Should a lawyer attend the sale? Do
you need an engineer's report?

Where is the sale held? Should you consider trying
to buy a property from the winning bidder? What
properties should you avoid? What additional costs
are involved in the purchase?

How should you handle refinancing questions?
What types of mortgage agreements are best for your
situation? How do you determine if you should have
a fixed-rate or an adjustable-rate mortgage?

What is the Resolution Trust Corporation, and what
should you know about it? Whom should you contact
about purchasing real estate that was once owned by
a savings and loan organization since gone bankrupt?

Why is buying an investment property different from
buying a home you plan to live in? How do you avoid
problem tenants?

Timely tips that will save you money and aggravation.

Should you use real estate brokers to help you sell?
What types of repair work will add the most value?

Too good to be true? Get the real lowdown and analysis.

Acknowledgments

I give grateful thanks to my daughter Constance, who made my hieroglyphics readable; to my son Richard, for his aid in assembling the manuscript and invaluable insights; to my wife Phyllis, for her patience, understanding, and editorial skill; to Bonita Nelson, who put it all together; and to my attorney Shepperd Daniels, whose wise counsel has guided me for over forty years.

Disclaimer

The sale and purchase of real estate falls within the purview of the Statute of Frauds. This provides that contracts regarding real estate, including transfers, must be in writing.

Since contracts involve laws of countries, states, and municipalities, it is recommended that you seek legal counsel. In my writings I touch upon subjects that could vary in different parts of the United States. I do not vouch for the legality of my opinions, nor is there an intent to supply legal advice.

Before taking action on my words, check with your attorney.

Foreword

It has become a cliché to view home ownership as the American Dream, but there is still truth in it.

Prior to World War II, the majority of Americans lived in rented lodging. Then the returning veterans found themselves setting up house in crowded cities; in many parts of the country, rent-controlled housing led to massive housing shortages. Through government initiatives such as the GI Bill and the new Federal Housing Administration (FHA), people who had only dreamed of home ownership were able to purchase housing. For as little as no cash down (through the Veterans Administration—the low-end commitment was typically 3 percent through the FHA), the entire country seemed to open up in a broad-based expansion of single-family home ownership.

Suddenly free from the constraints of cramped apartments, limited facilities, and a tight economy, families mushroomed. The baby boom began, a generation (born between 1946 and 1964) that never knew the restrained, austere lifestyles to which its parents had been subjected. The nation's overall standard of living increased dramatically in the years that followed World War II; in time, many baby boomers became yuppies—and became homeowners as well. The housing prices that greeted these buyers, although comparatively higher than those faced by their parents, were still within reach of these more affluent, career-minded homebuyers.

Now it is the baby boomers' children who have reached or are fast approaching the point at which they must leave the nest. These prospective homebuyers often face a significant challenge when it comes to purchasing their own homes. Broad-based changes in the real estate industry have served to put affordable, first-time housing on the endangered list.

Today's housing prices, even those for units purportedly designed for first-time buyers, are often completely unmanageable for the most recent wave of prospective homeowners. It is not the purpose of this book to examine why this has come about, but rather to explore one possible option for making homebuying more affordable, both for those who buy to obtain their own domicile and those who speculate: taking advantage of property foreclosures.

I should begin by pointing out that buying foreclosures is not the answer for everyone. It is unlikely that anything on the horizon today—and least of all the intelligent purchase of foreclosures—will affect the real estate industry to the same degree that the GI Bill and 3 percent Federal Housing Administration arrangements did. But if you are in search of affordable housing and are willing to do a good deal of legwork, this book may represent a real boon for you. And if you are interested in foreclosures as investment vehicles, I will venture that you will find this book a source of accurate and useful information.

I've been in the real estate industry for over fifty years. I learned many years ago that there really is no such thing as a free lunch; the old bromide about luck being the combination of preparation and opportunity is as true in my business as in any other.

Please don't begin this book with the impression that I am trying to dissuade you from taking advantage of the purchase of foreclosures! My only goal is to be sure you know that there will be effort required on your part to track down the remarkable values that are waiting for you in this field. That having been said, I'll close these remarks by noting that, as far as I'm concerned, real estate remains the greatest of all investments. If, by passing along suggestions arising from my own experience in this area, I can help you achieve your goals, then this undertaking will have been a success for both of us.

T. D.

CHAPTER ONE

How Foreclosures Happen

The word "foreclosure" means "to stop" or "to prevent." Today we are familiar with the word primarily because of its use with reference to mortgages. In law, to foreclose a mortgage means to cut off a borrower (also called a "mortgagor") from his right to redeem a property. Foreclosure provides the legal means by which a property owner may be stripped of that property because of his failure to live up to the terms of the contract he made when he borrowed money and pledged his real property as security for the loan.

Now then—a word about banks and mortgages. Banks do not give mortgages. That is surprising to many people, but it is nevertheless true. Banks loan money and *take back* mortgages as security for the loan. Thus, if your friend tells you that he "got a mortgage from the XYZ Savings Bank," he may be using the accepted parlance to describe the exchange that has taken place, but he is not quite correct. This is an important point to bear in mind, for reasons that will become clear as we go on in this chapter.

Purchase money mortgages are usually signed at a closing where the seller simultaneously gives a deed to the purchaser. At that time, the purchaser executes papers that are then given to the title company representative, who sees that they are recorded in the local county clerk's office. Of course, the papers being recorded are the deed to the property and the mortgage papers, which pledge the property as security for the loan.

The party doing the mortgaging or pledging is the new owner—and, in this instance, he becomes the *mortgagor.* The bank, which is the one to whom the property is pledged, becomes the *mortgagee.* People often confuse these terms because they regard the bank as the one owning the mortgage.

Many of the words used in real estate have their roots in English law, which was in turn based on Roman law. In Latin, "or" denotes a person performing an action; "ee" is the one receiving the action. Hence such terms as mortgagor/mortgagee, grantor/grantee, offeror/offeree, and so on, are all common in real estate transactions. We will be referring to mortgagors and mortgagees quite a bit in this book. I hope this brief summary has cleared up for you which is which; if you need to review the last few paragraphs before proceeding, please feel free to do so.

Although the underlying principles extend back to English Common Law, today's foreclosure procedures can be affected by state, county, and even local municipality laws. Unfortunately, there is no national code for foreclosures; things would be a great deal simpler if there were! If you are going to get involved in purchasing at foreclosure sales, it is absolutely imperative that you research the local laws. What follows in this book is an outline of the procedures in most localities, but there can be—and are—many local variations.

You could inquire of local attorneys about what to look for in purchasing foreclosed properties. Alternatively, you could consult a knowledgeable real estate broker in your area. A word of caution is in order here, however. Make sure your "expert" really is an expert in the field you need to learn about. An attorney who specializes in real estate *may* be able to help you— but he may also be essentially ignorant of foreclosure proceedings if these are not his specialty.

People are not likely to volunteer that they do not know something; this is a common human failing and one you must be wary of. No doubt you've had the experience of stopping to ask someone directions—only to find that you've been led well out of your way, although with the best intentions. How much better if the person had told you that he simply didn't know! My experience with attorneys is that they will seldom admit when they are unqualified to offer advice in a given area and will often offer advice that they *believe* to be correct, but that is in fact completely different from the advice you might have obtained from a more knowledgeable practitioner.

What other persons can you consult about local variations in foreclosure procedures? The clerk of the court is an excellent bet. If you can get him or her to talk to you, you'll very likely get some very sound advice. Some of these officials regard themselves as servants of the public and are an invaluable resource. Others will be more difficult to talk to. If you can find a clerk who is willing to share his or her expertise, you will likely get assistance from that clerk's staff, as well. This can be an invaluable aid.

Making sense of the terminology

In some states, there are *mortgages*. In others, there are *deeds of trust*. A deed of trust differs from a mortgage in that the trustor (borrower) hypothecates his legal title on the property to a *trustee* who is the actual legal title holder—while the debt obligation exists. The process is a pledge of the property to a third party, in order to ensure that you, the borrower, will make the payments as agreed.

The deed of trust is an instrument favored by banks since it makes applying the foreclosure process considerably easier should the need arise to do so. No judicial approval is required to begin foreclosure; in effect, the receiver (a term we'll learn more about later) is already appointed. In many areas, the deed of trust carries with it something called the "right of redemption."

Right of redemption is a process whereby the defaulting mortgagor can regain title to the property by fulfilling specific legal requirements. Although the property has been foreclosed, this foreclosure is revocable and can be overturned. The process is similar to an appeal. Rights of redemption exist only in certain specific instances; we'll review them later in the book.

In post–World War II real estate, the mortgage form most widely used was the one approved by the Federal Housing Administration. It is in these forms that the power to remove persons from title through the foreclosure process is established.

There are five covenants in the mortgage instrument you should know about. (The word "covenant" means "promise" or "agreement.")

The Five Covenants in a Mortgage

1. Mortgagor promises to pay the principal mortgage debt.
2. Mortgagor will keep building insured against fire for the benefit of the mortgagee.
3. No building will be demolished or removed without the consent of the mortgagee.
4. The entire principal will become due in the event of default of payment of principal, interest, taxes, or assessments.
5. The mortgagor will consent to the appointment of a receiver in the event of a foreclosure.

These five covenants have received virtually universal acceptance among savings banks and savings and loan institutions.

The first three are agreements that the mortgagor must adhere to; in the event that these agreements are breached, the other two covenants are options that the mortgagee must pursue. Why "must"? Mortgagees are really trust officers. The money they've loaned you is not theirs. It belongs to their depositors; mortgagees have no right to take risks with other people's money. They must, therefore, stick to the letter of the agreement.

These last two covenants give the bank the means to foreclose. One provides for the appointment of a receiver; the other provides that, in the event of default, the bank can accelerate payments and ask for the entire balance. The accelerating payment covenant is of great importance to the bank. If it didn't have such a provision, it would be in court continuously, suing for three or four back payments at a time, then repeating the procedure. In essence, when the bank's lawyers take someone to court, they want all of the money; if it can't be paid, they want a judgment against the mortgagor. Until the time that judgment is obtained, the mortgagor really is under no threat of foreclosure. But once the judgment has been handed down, the mortgagor has had his day in court—and can be put out of the property.

Forbearance provisions and deeds in lieu of foreclosure

Of course, this book is meant for those who are looking to buy property at foreclosure in the hope of finding a suitable abode at an affordable price, or for those who want to pick up properties at a low price and resell them at a higher price. I mention this because it's possible that someone in financial difficulty may be reading this in hopes of finding some miraculous means of halting the foreclosure process. While such problems are not the main focus of this book, a few words are probably in order about the perspective of the original homeowner in this situation.

The Federal Housing Administration has a program—which the FHA alone may invoke—to help a mortgagor who is in temporary difficulty. It is called a *forbearance provision.* Under this arrangement, the mortgagor would ask the FHA to agree to a schedule whereby the mortgagor could pay a portion of the money owed—provided the terms are acceptable to all parties. Subsequent payments would then be made directly to the FHA. In these cases, the FHA replaces the banks—and usually has a local representative who follows up and represents the FHA as a local property manager.

Even though they are obliged to do so under certain conditions, banks operating in today's financial climate are hesitant to initiate foreclosures. Unlike in past years, banks face a growing number of foreclosures, and they are likely to want to work with their customers to head off problems before they become serious. So a call from a borrower in trouble is likely to go a long way.

If there is no way out, and the only legal claim the mortgagor has against his credit is the lack of bank payments, he is well advised to explore the process of a *deed in lieu of foreclosure*. Under this process, the mortgagor might be able to work out a temporary rental agreement with the bank—which would be the new owner of the property. With a deed in lieu of foreclosure, the mortgagor asks the bank to accept a deed, since he may not be able to make payments as agreed and would like to get out of the mortgage contract as gracefully as possible.

In many instances, the homeowner has moved to another city (often as a result of a work transfer) and has simply been unable to sell the property. He is willing to forego any equity he holds; he wants out. As long as there are no other liens against the property, the procedure described above probably represents the best avenue for the bank to take. After all, pursuing the foreclosure process would involve a whole host of expenses that can be eliminated outright by accepting a deed directly from the mortgagor. The advantage for the mortgagor is that he walks away with his credit intact and future real estate purchases will not be hindered as a result of the episode. It may not be an ideal situation, but each side can come away with a win of sorts.

I will explain this type of transfer in greater detail in a following chapter.

Selling the property

After a judgment is handed down against the mortgagor, a time is selected for the public sale of the property. If the mortgagor cannot redeem the amount of the judgment award before the sale, that's it. No more delays, no more compromises; the sale will be held.

You will remember that one of the covenants we examined earlier had to do with the appointment of a receiver; this is where that provision comes into play. The court can appoint someone (usually a lawyer) to conduct the sale of the mortgagor's property. That person is known as the receiver.

Ordinarily, real property cannot be transferred unless both grantees (purchasers) in the purchase deed sign the new transfer deed. Of course, no one who is having his home taken away is going to volunteer to sign a deed over to someone else. The receiver has the authority (granted by the court) to sign a valid deed transferring the ownership to a new purchaser.

What are the root causes of foreclosure proceedings?

Why, exactly, do foreclosures come about?

The two biggest reasons are marital discord and business failures. To be sure, there are also cases where people lose jobs and bills pile up, but these are not the typical foreclosure cases. In such situations, people will usually make remarkable efforts to weather the adverse conditions: refinancing the debt, taking a second job, or—in the case of a spouse who had previously not worked—finding employment for the first time.

The most common reason for foreclosure is dissolution of a marriage, generally involving abandonment by the husband.

The next most common reason for foreclosure is the once-promising business venture that fails. In these cases, the homeowner is usually mortgaged to the hilt and has been completely overwhelmed by debts. Foreclosure is usually the only option available to the bank in such a situation.

In years past, when people found themselves in serious financial difficulty, they were able to sell off their home or refinance the mortgage in order to consolidate debts. In this way, they were able to combine many smaller loans with high monthly payments into one debt and reduce their monthly outlay. They might even be able to pay off many of the debts and scale down to a smaller home with a more manageable monthly payment. This solution is less common today for one main reason: home prices have fallen sharply in many regions. In case after case, the existing indebtedness simply exceeds the present market value of the home; foreclosure is the only solution.

This trend is leading to a plethora of bank-owned properties. That is the result of a foreclosure sale that produces no buyers! If there are no buyers at the sale, the bank becomes the owner. From this point on, the bank is free to make whatever deal it wants.

"Why can't they work with me?"

Perhaps the hardest thing for a defaulting mortgagor to understand is the bank's refusal to accept partial payments. But this really is not a solution to the problem. If the bank accepts partial payment on a home loan in default, it establishes as accepted procedure something that is completely contrary to sound banking practice. Furthermore, if it can be established in a future legal action that the bank has in the past accepted partial payments, the court might hold the practice to be acceptable and decide that the bank's action constitutes a waiver.

Remember, the legal process is based on law, but is subject to interpretation of that law. In contractual relationships, it is very common for courts to view the failure to pursue the due process of an agreement as a waiver. Bankers don't want to open the floodgates in this area; they are quite insistent about following the mortgaging agreement to the letter when faced with a clear-cut case in which foreclosure is in order.

The bank's point of view on such matters often comes as a surprise to laymen. For instance, banks really don't like collecting late charges—even though doing so would seem to represent a financial advantage for them. But the reality is that a high percentage of late payments is a sign of a sloppy operation. Banks want to know that payments are received on time; their business is predicated on the use of money they receive at certain predetermined intervals. If they don't receive the money on time, the business will not be run as efficiently as it should.

Banks, we must remember, are in a fiduciary position. That means they are trustees of the money their depositors leave with them. Banks must be accountable at all times to the people who have placed their trust in them.

Perhaps the past rash of abuses in the savings and loan industry makes you question the accuracy of the foregoing. The fact is, scavengers exist in all walks of life, and business and government are no exception. The fact that there are bad examples does not mean that abuse is standard practice. There will be instances of misconduct, but on the whole the principles of operation remain sound. Most financial institutions act as the trustees that they are.

CHAPTER TWO

The Foreclosure Proceedings

The melodramas of a bygone age depicted a Simon Legree–type of mortgagee who wanted nothing more than to wrest the old homestead from Little Nell and her poor elderly parents. The cliché has now become quite familiar: the mustache-twirling villain who says, "Pay the mortgage by five today—or else!" The impression left with the audience was that the cold-hearted man had given the loan solely for the opportunity of stealing the old homestead away from the poor-but-honest landholders.

Then there's the stereotype of the Western power broker whose goal was to accumulate land so he could exercise political power over the entire community. You probably remember the fellow in those old late-show westerns wearing the black hat. This villain was usually surrounded by a covey of evil-looking henchmen who gloated at news of blight, fire, or other devastation, gleeful at the opportunity to snatch land from unfortunate farmers. Here, too, the idea was apparently to give the loan only to have the chance to take over the security in case of default.

These stereotypes have been circulated widely; they work much better as entertainment than they do as models for sound financial practice. The conventional sources of mortgage financing—banks and savings and loan institutions—are interested in good investment return on good investment risks secured by good investment property. When they are compelled to foreclose and take a property back, that is an indication that a serious mistake has been made. Most businesspeople know from personal experience that mistakes can be quite costly; no one goes out of his way to allow one to occur.

Let me qualify that: There may be a few mortgagees whose interest in granting loans is to await the default and then acquire the property through foreclosure, but they are very much the exception to the rule. Most lenders who loan money under riskier-than-normal conditions are looking for a higher-than-normal rate of return.

This brings us to one of the primary axioms of investing, which goes as follows: The greater the risk, the higher the return. Agencies that grant mortgage loans where the faint-hearted will not are usually referred to as "hard money" lenders. These individuals will take greater risks—for a price. They want a markedly higher return on their investment. However, as a broad—but reliable—rule, they do not want to acquire the property.

Too many people forget that banks are selling a commodity. That commodity is called "money." It may be difficult to think of money as a commodity, but that is nevertheless what it is. Money is bought, sold, traded, exchanged, and assigned. When we go to the bank, hat in hand, to ask for a loan, what we are doing is asking the bank to permit us buy the product it sells.

Do you walk into a retail store and ask, "Won't you please take a moment out of your busy schedule and allow me to buy a pound of sugar from your store?" Of course not. Well, that situation is essentially no different from the one you face at the bank when seeking to borrow money. At the end of each day, the loan officer goes into his boss's office and boasts, "I just gave out two million dollars today!" The boss replies, "That's great, George. Keep up the good work and we'll break last month's record."

Given the way mortgage banking is set up today, there is no shortage of mortgage money out there. There are a number of reasons for this.

Although you make your payment to the Penny Savings Bank, it is not really the mortgagee. Most of the money being loaned today is being sold off in what's known as the "secondary market." This is the alphabetical melange you've heard referred to as Fannie Mae and Freddie Mac. These quasigovernmental agencies are the *Federal National Mortgage Administration* and the *Federal Home Loan Mortgage Corporation*. These are public offerings sold by public subscription through stockbrokers. You may have heard someone say something along the lines of, "Invest in Ginnie Maes; they're high-yield investments secured by real property." What is really being described are the mortgages that are originated by most banks.

The public purchases these offerings; the resulting money is the source for new mortgage agreements. In years past, savings banks could allocate a set amount for mortgage purposes each year. At the beginning of the year, they were more generous in their approvals and amounts being offered. As the year progressed and the allocated sums were being exhausted, the banks would retrench and refuse loans or offer lesser amounts in order to stretch funds further. Today, that problem is alleviated; the mortgages are being sold in the secondary market to Fannie Mae and Freddie Mac.

But why, you may ask, are you making your payments to the Penny Savings Bank? The answer is that it has retained the servicing of the mortgage for a fee. That's why the loan officer is so happy when he tells his boss about two million more dollars going out the door. As a businessperson, how would you feel about your organization receiving one-half percent per month of each new loan, with more loans being made each day? It adds up!

You may also have heard of something called the "float." That's the period of time that money (for instance, your mortgage payment) passes through a bank and does not incur any outside expenses. This, too, adds up, and is another reason banks really do want to lend to you: you're helping them just as much as they're helping you. However, if you don't make your payments on time, they have to send their money to Fanny and Freddy; they're not floating your money, they're paying your debts.

This should serve to illustrate why the worst thing you can have on a credit report (from a bank's point of view, at any rate) is a history of chronic late mortgage payments. Banks who see this profile don't want to know any more. They can make their decision immediately: No!

Many people feel this is unfair. "After all," they say, "I do pay up. I may not pay right on time, but I've never received a lawyer's letter. They've never had to chase after me." Stop and think, though: If you were a landlord with a mortgage to pay, would you be happy shelling out money to the bank each month without having received your rent?

Receiving a letter from a lawyer is a sign, not of having committed a minor oversight that the bank wants corrected, but of having entered into the realm of the serious problem debtor. If you get a letter from a lawyer, you are in trouble. Lawyers don't do anything without being compensated, and rightly so. When you hear from a lawyer, it means the bank has decided to commit its resources to the problem of getting you to pay the money you owe on time.

The stages of foreclosure

From this point onward, let us assume you are a homeowner having financial problems. Exactly how will the foreclosure proceed?

Well, when you call the lawyer to explain why you haven't paid, you will not receive much sympathy. The lawyer is there to protect the bank's interest, period. Many mortgagors believe the lawyer should be able to at least show some understanding of the circumstances surrounding the back money owed. He won't. He is interested in one topic only: when you intend to pay up.

If you can't make an agreement with the lawyer, you will be on your way to the first stage of foreclosure. You will be served with a summons. After service (the process by which you are physically presented with the summons), the attorney will file papers with the county clerk. (In this book I will refer to the county clerk's office frequently, although in some areas the place where deeds and mortgages are registered may go by a different name, such as the office of the land registrar.) This notice is usually known as *Lis Pendens,* which is Latin for "pending legal action."

Now your credit is a matter of public record. All the credit reporting services will have access to the current status of your debt, as will anyone who consults the records of the county clerk. There are publications that publish all the Lis Pendens filed in a given area, and these will list not only the bank's filing against you, but also those of any of your other creditors who have filed.

Your mortgage payment record is now out in the open and in the files of numerous credit reporting bureaus. (Unlike instances of Lis Pendens, late payments to a bank don't normally show up on a credit report unless specifically requested of the mortgagee by the credit reporting organization.) At this point, any attempt you make to borrow from public credit sources will be met with a negative response.

When the attorney decided to go ahead with the foreclosure action, he asked his title company to prepare a search. Since the deed and mortgage are typically recorded at the same time, the mortgage is usually the first obligation against the property. If the title company that recorded it delayed the recording of the mortgage for some reason, it's possible that something could have been recorded against the former owner—or even the present owner—during that interim period. (The recording company would be responsible in such a case.)

For our purposes, however, we will assume that the first claim against the property is the mortgage. Any subsequent mortgages, judgments, or liens (other than tax liens) are classified as junior obligations. All of these parties must be served with papers in the foreclosure action so that they may have the right to bid in to protect their interest.

The Lis Pendens papers will join all of them as defendants; all their names will become part of the public record relative to this case. In other words, it will be public knowledge that you owe money to, and have not paid, all the parties. If the foreclosing party was negligent in notifying the junior lien holders, those creditors not joined in the action would have a valid claim for repayment against the new owner.

Could such a claim affect someone who purchases the property at the foreclosure auction? Yes! That's why title insurance is essential.

To enforce money judgments, the defaulting parties must be served personally. That's one of the main reasons foreclosure actions take so long—the mortgagor must be tracked down and handed a piece of paper. Often, the mortgagor will not want to be served. In other cases, such as that of the husband who has left his wife and family, the problem becomes even more complex.

How is such an issue resolved? Each jurisdiction has its own laws and rules. Generally, if a person cannot be located, and if all reasonable efforts have been made to find him, a procedure for publication will suffice. This consists of a public notice printed in the classified section of the local newspaper; no doubt you have seen such notices yourself.

Most jurisdictions require public notice whether or not the mortgagor(s) have been served. This is to put the public on notice that the property is to be foreclosed and that parties with a legitimate claim against the property should come forth.

On completion of the publication process, the foreclosure action will be permitted to proceed. In many instances, the mortgagors have left the premises and have rented the property to tenants from whom they have been receiving (and pocketing) rent payments. If the names of these tenants are known, the action will stipulate them in the notice. If the names are not known, the tenants will be served as John Doe and/or Jane Doe.

As a general rule, tenants of a building that is being foreclosed enjoy no special rights to remain. Most standard leases provide that the premises must be vacated in the event of foreclosure. Many of these tenants took the property on a lease purchase option, with option money paid to the defaulting mortgagor. These people are, quite frankly, in a very unfortunate position. They have a right of action against the landlord, of course, but at this stage he or she is likely to have other problems—e.g., the money owed to the bank and other creditors—and is not the best target for a successful lawsuit.

In my fifty-plus years in the real estate business, I've run across a number of shady characters who've taken over properties by one means or another from troubled owners, then turned around and rented them out at what appeared to be a terrific value. They collected the rents for as long as they could, paid the mortgagee nothing, and laughed all the way to the bank. Such episodes only reinforce a valuable principle: If something looks too good to be true, it probably is. That goes for any number of "dream" real estate deals you may come across. Ask for references if you have any doubts about the propriety of an agreement or offer.

Are you getting what you think you're getting?

A notice of a foreclosure sale sets forth all the creditors, but you really won't know from the text alone whether it's describing a first mortgage lien or a second mortgage lien. If it appears that a relatively small mortgage on a fantastic piece of property is being offered, go to the county clerk's office and ask to see the recorded papers. The terms of the sale will be recorded there.

The terms of the sale will tell you if there are any prior mortgages. If you purchase a junior mortgage lien, you are acquiring it subject to the first mortgage lien. Let's take a look at an example of how this might work. You may buy what appears to be a $250,000 house for a $50,000 foreclosure bid and find that there's a $170,000 first mortgage on it, which you now own as well. It may very well be that the first mortgage is in serious default, and if you don't bring it up to date, you'll be out of title soon as well!

A "due on sale" mortgage acquired by the foreclosure process is transferable; you won't be called in to pay it up or replace it. (We'll discuss this type of mortgage in more detail later on in the book.)

With the advent of "home equity" mortgages, which are usually second mortgages, you'll find that a lot of those foreclosure actions involving "bargain" amount sums on quality properties are dated from 1986 forward. The chances are very good that such proceedings represent defaulted second mortgages. On the other hand, if a foreclosure action shows a mortgage origination date of 1972 or some such other distant date, you can count on its being a first mortgage and worthy of your attention.

The notices of the pending foreclosure will often show the names of the mortgagor's attorney and receiver. They usually will not yield all the information you might like about the proceeding; all they will disclose is whether and when the sale will be held, or if it has been adjourned for some reason.

If you call the offices of the attorneys mentioned in the notice, you may find yourself annoyed at how uncooperative the secretaries seem to be with regard to answering your queries.

Remember that a law office exists to provide legal services; that is all. The staff at the office may or may not know the answers to your questions, but if they were to answer all the public calls they get about the sale, they wouldn't get their own work done. They are being paid, not to provide hotline service, but to prepare the papers and conduct the sale.

The obligation to determine the priority of the lien is yours. If the property sounds promising to you, do the research or have it done for you. You can go to the county clerk's office and conduct a title search yourself, but you are probably better advised to pay the minimal fee necessary to have a professional do the job. There is a small army of researchers who are familiar with the filing systems and personnel at the various facilities; these researchers can usually be found through referrals from the offices of the county clerk. Another option is to have a local attorney conduct the search for you. Either approach represents a minimal investment that is probably worthwhile, considering the potential damage that can be done to your interests if there is a "cloud on the title"—a gap in the chain of ownership or an unpaid tax assessment or other lien.

If you're a novice who is doing this for the first time, you must be mindful of the position of the mortgage that's being foreclosed. If it isn't a first mortgage, then there are possibly other mortgages or recorded judgments that predate the subject mortgage.

Hiring someone to research the property for you is risky because you may not be the prevailing bidder and you've spent for naught. Go to the Recording Office and ask the clerk about the procedure. He or she will probably be very happy to help you. That's part of the job and you needn't feel guilty about asking for help.

CHAPTER THREE

Contacting Mortgagors Prior to the Sale

Let's assume that your aim is to purchase a home for yourself. If you become aware of someone in financial difficulty in an area where you'd like to live, you would do well to contact the mortgagor directly. By contact directly, I mean just that: Go to the house, knock on the door, and speak to the people face-to-face. Don't rely on the phone.

If a Lis Pendens has been filed, chances are that the mortgagors have been contacted by local real estate outfits and investors. As someone who simply wants to buy the home as a domicile, you stand a better chance than they do because homeowners in financial difficulty are likely to feel that the investors and brokers are "out to steal" their home.

This is why I am advising you to go straight to the door. Let them see you, meet you, and learn that you are not in the business of buying or selling homes. They'll feel safer dealing with you.

After all, an investor or broker speaking to a homeowner is approaching the person on what is basically a "wholesale" purchase. He will be looking to turn it over for a profit; you, as a user, will be prepared to pay a somewhat higher price. Your message will have an easier time getting through.

How do you find properties that are facing foreclosure?

One way is to go to the county clerk's office and read the postings.

Another method is to follow the published notices in the newspapers. If you're interested in a particular location, you'd do well to buy the local weekly publication for that area. If there's a foreclosure in that town, the chances are good that it will be published in the local weekly.

When you read the notice in the local paper, it will feature the name of the bank's attorney. Let me caution you once again not to attempt to call this person for information about the sale. You're probably better off calling the bank directly; ask to speak to someone in the delinquent mortgage section. Even here, however, you should be resigned to the fact that people will not go out of their way to get information for you. The reason I am proposing you call the bank at all is that it is possible someone may know the case well and be able—and willing—to pass along information requiring no research to unearth. In the end, however, there is really no substitute for your own efforts at the property or the county registrar's office.

Lease arrangements

If you are an investor and you encounter a situation where the party is a solid citizen, one approach you might take is to purchase the property and lease it back at a rental that will cover the mortgage payment plus a fair return on your investment.

"Defaulting party" and "solid citizen" may at first appear to be contradictory. There are times when individuals who actually represent very good risks are incapable of obtaining refinancing through more conventional means due to unusual circumstances or temporary setbacks. In such a case, you will have to make your own judgment and decide accordingly.

At any rate, in these circumstances you will own the home; the prior owners are tenants who are renting with an option to buy. The title will be in your name; you will have assumed the mortgage. You will have taken the deed from the prior owners and signed a lease with them that will give them an option to purchase; they are now tenants and subject to the provisions of a valid lease. If they don't pay under these conditions, the removal process is not the cumbersome one of foreclosure. When tenants don't pay rent, the procedure available to you is the simpler one of eviction.

The option purchase price should be the same price you paid for the property. If you give them a higher price, you could be guilty of usury. Current case law illustrates that setting an option to purchase at a later date and at a higher price constitutes exceeding the legal rate of interest.

But why go to the trouble at all if you can't charge more? In these circumstances, the sum you pay to bring the mortgage current plus the existing mortgage balance should be far below the value of the property. (If it isn't, don't buy in the first place.)

As we have seen, if your new tenants default, you are the owner of a bargain property. If they stick to their word and make the payments, you're getting a very healthy return on your money—plus twelve or twenty-four months amortization on the mortgage, which increases your yield.

In the event of acquisition, you've also saved closing costs, since the bank has already gone along with the transfer of the mortgage. It's a great deal for you either way.

Let me offer a scenario that should show exactly how this process can work.

Let's assume that the property is worth, in your opinion, about $150,000. There is a first mortgage of $90,000, with monthly payments of $1,050 including principal, interest, taxes, and fire insurance. The homeowner needs $6,000 to bring his mortgage current—and has other loans on which he is in arrears that total $14,000. This makes a total need of $20,000.

You bring the mortgage current and pay off the debts, which had monthly payments totaling $650. You take a deed and give him a lease with an option to purchase the property in a year at a price of $110,000—which is what you paid for it. ($90,000 + $20,000 = $110,000.)

At this point he has been paying $1,050 plus $650 on his debts, for a total of $1,700. Your rental figure will be based on the $1,050, plus a respectable interest return on your money.

Consider: You've paid out $20,000 plus costs for abstracts, recording, and legal services of $1,500; the total here comes to $21,500. You want 12 percent on your money, which is 1 percent per month. On that basis, you would need $215, plus $1,050 to pay the mortgage. That means, in this case, a monthly rental of $1,265, which would probably be a reasonable rent. (Even if you wanted 15 percent on your money, or 1 1/4 percent per month, that would be $268.75 plus $1,050, or $1,318.75, which even if higher than the going rental rate is likely to be acceptable to your new tenant under the circumstances.)

The rental rate has nothing to do with usury or anything else. It's a lease—not a purchase. Options are paid for by investors all over the world. This usually involves a good faith deposit, which is forfeited if the option is not exercised. In this case, you've given him an option to buy; it is not necessary to consider the additional rent as an option.

Basically, you're giving the person a chance to get out of a hole. You've cleaned up his indebtedness, reduced his monthly charges, and provided him with a chance to get back on his feet.

If you stop and analyze the transaction I'm suggesting, you'll see it really isn't a true sale. You're loaning money to stop the foreclosure, then giving the person a chance to pay you back. Of course, if he defaults on the lease, you can evict for nonpayment, and the house is yours, clear of any encumbrance. (As we will soon see, however, you are best advised to spell all this out—specifically, the fact that the option to buy the home is canceled if rent is not kept current—with absolute clarity in your agreement.)

You have an excellent chance to own a house for less than its true value, in these cases. Don't let it appear that you are looking to do him out of his home through a tricky device.

If the term is for one or two years and he is not prepared to go through with the purchase, extend the term for one more year. When the final expiration is over, he can't accuse you of any wrongs. You have bent over backwards to help him. He is the defaulter, not you.

"Due on sale" clauses

In instituting the leasing arrangement I've described, there is a problem you might run into—one that has to do not with the mortgagor, but rather with the mortgagee: the "due on sale" clause. If you encounter this clause, you are best advised to visit the bank and talk with the officials there about your proposal to buy the property.

A "due on sale" clause guarantees the bank the right to demand all moneys owed it when the property changes hands. The clause was first instituted some decades back because, although interest rates had risen substantially over the years, existing mortgages were being transferred with no approval needed—and with interest rates well below the current market. Older mortgages, particularly those that were VA-guaranteed or FHA-insured, were being transferred to new owners at older, lower rates of interest—with no credit check. With a "due on sale" provision, banks could ask for a higher rate and approve the creditworthiness of the new purchaser.

If you are creditworthy and are attempting to set up the kind of leasing arrangement I am describing here, the bank will probably approve the arrangement and waive the clause. It is possible that the rate of interest it is currently receiving is in today's range. If you can offer the bank the hope of avoiding a foreclosure and commit believably to making all the payments yourself, you will probably be seen as a knight in shining armor. That's one less foreclosure to make.

Speak to the bank about transferring the mortgage to you. The likelihood is that, given today's environment, the bank will listen to you happily.

Who will you be dealing with?

People facing foreclosure fall into several categories. Let's take a look at a few of them here.

We spoke earlier of the absentee husband who takes off and leaves the family to fend for itself. Unfortunately, there's usually nothing you can do for the unfortunate wife. Any transfer of property would require both signatures, and that's not going to happen if the husband is nowhere to be found. When banks face a situation like this, they accept that the foreclosure process is going to take some time.

All you can really do in this case is to keep in touch with the bank and monitor the progress of the foreclosure. Eventually, all the formalities of the judicial process will have been advanced, and the sale will take place.

Another category is the businessperson whose once-promising venture has fallen flat. The reaction here to your offer to buy the property is likely to be one of interest. After all, you are offering the individual—who is probably quite familiar by now with dire warnings from authorities concerning unpaid debts—a way out that is more in the socially acceptable order of things. So you stand a good chance of being heard out, at the very least.

Of course, individual reactions will vary. You will also have to take into account that this person has probably been under a good deal of stress in recent months. Tact and an easygoing, nonthreatening manner are essential.

A third category is the mortgagor who has simply never learned fiscal responsibility. An era of easy credit has made him a voracious consumer, and by that I mean he will simply keep consuming as long as people will permit him to consume. One day he discovers that the people who extended him the easy credit want to be repaid.

The main problem with him is identifying all the potential obstacles to your purchase of the property. When you first start your discussions with him, he'll likely tell you that all he owes is his mortgage and his credit cards. But if you take the effort to probe and ask whether he owes anything to, for instance, Household Finance, you may get an "Oh, yeah, that's right" kind of response. With this person, it will be wise for you to learn how to check the judgment rolls in the county clerk's office. You might then find that those finance company debts are judgments—and that there's one from the phone company and one from an insurance broker as well. Rule number one with this person: Do not give him one red cent before all searches are completed, title insurance is purchased, and all necessary papers are signed by the parties in interest. Not a down payment, not a hundred-dollar gesture of good faith, nothing. (Your best bet is to deal exclusively with an attorney representing this individual.)

Why you are in the driver's seat

Remember, you're dealing with a situation that will deprive a person of the right to live within his home. That may be an extreme idea to most people, but to the courts and authorities it's simple enough. The mortgagee hasn't been paid, and there is a binding contract—the mortgage agreement—that states exactly what is to happen under that set of circumstances. The contract says, in essence, "I'm loaning you money; you have to repay me or I can take action to enforce my claim by foreclosing on the property. If you agree to this arrangement, sign here." The courts and authorities aren't particularly interested in whether or not this represents a pleasant development for all parties; if that really is the mortgagor's signature on the document, they are interested in disposing of the case as efficiently as possible. Sooner or later, the mortgagor will realize that.

What is an order to show cause?

At one time, I had a lot of rental properties and managed many of them personally. When I did not receive rent payments, I would invoke the judicial process. Invariably, I would get a default judgment, but before I could execute it, I would receive an order to show cause. Why? The tenant would go to the local Legal Aid Society with a tale of woe about how inadequate my facilities were (which was completely untrue); the legal stalwarts would then take me to court to make me prove why I was justified in evicting the tenant (in other words, "show cause"). They'd also describe all my purported ulterior motives for putting the tenant out. (Actually, the reason was always quite straightforward: he or she would not pay the rent.) Time after time, this amounted to nothing more than a delaying exercise; it never changed anything. But each time I was stuck with at least another month of no receipts and continuing expenses.

Your situation will be much different from mine, of course. You think you've bought a property, and you want to take possession. You may be asked to show why you are justified in doing so by the court through an order to show cause.

The agreement

If the mortgagor insists that he won't use an attorney in finalizing the sale of the property, you must incorporate a clause in your agreement that says that you have advised him that he should secure the services of counsel but has chosen not to do so.

Make the letter of agreement as clear as possible; spell everything out in the most obvious terms. Every component of your agreement must be in layman's language that is impossible to misunderstand, or as close as you can come to that standard. In the event of a later dispute, you will not be able to defend yourself effectively by saying, "I assumed he understood."

If you will be accepting payments from the mortgagor and allowing him to remain in the house, for instance, don't write about "foreclosure" or "dispossession." Write, "If you don't make the payments as agreed, I have the right to go to court and have the judge sign an order that will enable me to have you removed from the house. That means the sheriff will put your furniture out on the curb and you and your family as well." Blunt? Yes. But you must nevertheless write it in language that anyone will understand, then read it back and ask if it's clear and if there are any questions.

Since you are going to be an investor, you should not skimp on legal services. Obtain the services of a competent real estate attorney whose job will be to represent you. You can use this person as the escrow agent to hold your good faith deposit and to advise you in the event you encounter any difficulties. There are localities where lawyers do the title searches for the company that provides title insurance. In these areas, you may be able to secure the services of the attorney for just a little more than the cost of the search itself.

If there ever comes a time when you are asked to show cause in court, the fact that you used the services of an attorney in framing the agreement will definitely weigh in your favor. Remember, judges are lawyers; they have two reasons for preferring to see the agreement developed in concert with one of their own. First, they are less likely to come across serious errors or omissions if a lawyer has signed off on everything. Second, they are less likely to conclude that one party is taking advantage of another if there is a lawyer involved.

There are many areas of the country where people skip using lawyers when drafting sale agreements. For my part, I always use an attorney. People who ask whether they really need an attorney for this step remind me of people who ask whether you really need a doctor when you go into labor. Of course, more than one beat cop has delivered a baby, but if a complication arises, you do need a competent professional who knows what he's doing. How many people are certain that their situation will be completely free of complications?

You never know what will crop up in a real estate transaction. Include the services of an attorney in your cost acquisition figures.

Additions and improvements

People buy houses. Over the years they improve them by adding garages, extensions, decks, dormers, pools, and so on. In years past, the properties in question were sold without certificates of any sort to cover the added improvements. The sales were made, the mortgages were arranged, the title insurance was secured, and no one suffered any additional expense.

Those days are gone. The bank you obtain your mortgage from—and it may be the same one that holds the seller's mortgage—will want completion certificates for all additions because it now has to play by FNMA's (Fannie Mae's) rules.

FNMA wants completion certificates for everything that requires one according to the local zoning ordinances. The person occupying the house now probably doesn't know that, but you should. Since FNMA wants those certificates, your bank has to have them; since your bank has to have them, you have to get them from the person who's selling you the house.

It may not be that difficult in some cases. Often, all that is necessary is to file the plans, have the improvements inspected, and pay for the certificate. There are times, however, when the process is a little more complicated. For instance, you will occasionally encounter improvements that violate a zoning ordinance. You will then have two problems. First, it is very likely that you will have to wait a long time before any hearings are held on the matter, and even longer for a final decision. Second, the zoning board may not approve of the work and may ask that it be altered to conform to code.

Let's assume, though, for the sake of argument, that you do obtain a variance (permission to overlook existing code) from the board. You now have to have the improvement approved. Some of these actions require the notification of neighbors within a certain radius of the property; they may have the right to attend the relevant hearing and air their concerns. Can you imagine the next-door neighbor who's always objected to that ugly shed facing her property being told that there's going to be a hearing to determine if it can stand?

This is a nightmarish scenario, to be sure, and it is not at all uncommon. Such potential problems will certainly affect your strategy when you're looking to purchase from a defaulting mortgagor. If you're going to need a mortgage, you could be facing very serious obstacles. And even if you won't need a mortgage—in other words, if you were planning to purchase for resale—the chances are that your eventual purchaser *will* need one, and any problems obtaining one will hurt you, the seller.

So you must keep an eye out for any improvements that have been made to the property and ask the current mortgagor if he has certificates for same. There is still the difficulty that he may have one for the garage but nothing for the deck, yet he tells you he has "all the papers." The bottom line is that you should do yourself a favor and hike over to the municipality's building department to see what's on record.

There are firms that will draw plans and specifications for precisely these circumstances. They usually know the local zoning ordinances well and can look at the property and tell you what modifications, if any, are needed. You'll find it very easy to get free—and usually quite reliable—advice in this area since you are likely to use the services of the firm to obtain the permits and certificates once you've acquired the property.

The ordinary catch-up procedure is usually not a big problem; the long-undetected violations of zoning ordinances usually are. (I have seen decks torn out and new ones constructed as a result of these kinds of infractions.) You will have to weigh the pros and cons yourself before committing to the sale.

"Equity sharing"

One method of home sharing and ownership that is often proposed by the late-night television infomercial entrepreneurs is the "equity share" program. This idea is often advanced as a method for handling the party facing foreclosure. It is a bad idea. If you're going to be sharing a title with people who are constantly in financial hot water, you are asking for problems. Any judgments they incur can be attached to the property; that attachment is not in proportion to the other party's ownership.

It is completely against the property. Your newfound partner can strip you of all you own in the property by, for instance, borrowing from someone else, never repaying the loan, and having the case go to judgment.

Equity share programs are all right in certain circumstances but represent a huge no-no when dealing with a party facing foreclosure. These programs are for people who have good credit records but are low on cash. To put the matter bluntly, do you really want to go partners with someone you know to be a deadbeat?

The hard fact is, there are certain people in this world who just have a hard time handling money. When I managed rental properties, I often listened to the tales of woe and became convinced that unusual circumstances had a way of conspiring against basically good people. I tried to compensate by taking an extra month's security from tenants who seemed to have a history of financial problems. It never worked. They used it up. After a while, I noticed that the people who said, "Everything always happens to me!" were usually right.

There really is no precaution you can take against people who are bad credit risks. If you must deal with such a person, do what you have to do and get out. The longer you work with the individual, the more it will cost you.

Painful experience has shown me that these people are constantly in hot water; even if you solve their immediate problem, they'll be back in trouble next year, next month, and maybe even next week. Unless you're in a completely foolproof position (and who among us can boast of that?), don't get involved on a long-term basis.

You can empathize all you want—but don't sympathize. You can't afford to take their problems on as your own.

CHAPTER FOUR

Dealing with Banks

I said a little earlier that banks really do not want to acquire your property, that they would much prefer to concentrate on the business of selling or renting money. Once banks are put into the position of being property owners, they share the burdens, problems, and objectives of all the other people who own and want to sell property.

Homeowners are fond of saying things like "The bank still owns half of this place." Let's remember that although the bank's mortgage loan is generally far in excess of the mortgagor's equity in the property, the bank really does not own the house—until a foreclosure situation develops. At that point, the bank *does* have to take over things like watering the lawn, cutting the grass, fixing the rain spouts, and the hundred and one other chores that homeowners must perform. And that's not really the bank's idea of the ideal job. But when the banker

---

35

moves into title through the foreclosing process, he owns the property and must see that such work is done.

Many banks have a property management officer who has the responsibility of safeguarding properties. Some banks employ property management concerns, usually local real estate brokers who provide the services for a fee. Of course, that's a fee the bank would rather not have to pay. If the property is damaged through vandalism or natural causes, the banks have to decide what to do in response. Those aren't the kinds of decisions bankers are trained to make, and focusing on such issues detracts from the day-to-day fulfillment of bank duties.

There is a big difference between regular sellers and bank sellers: Banks are not permitted to make a profit on real estate sales!

It should be abundantly clear, then, that the bank really has no interest in foreclosing on your property. When a bank has to do so, it adds a new obligation to the debit side of the financial statement. That debit is known as "owned real estate," often referred to as ORE. Bankers hate to have this show up in their statements. ORE represents loans that went sour, even though all the most conservative standards were applied in the consideration of the original application.

"How on earth did this happen?"

Bankers would seem to have as much reason to ask this kind of question as the defaulting mortgagor. One of the primary reasons the bank finds itself in title is that no one has offered to buy the house at the foreclosure sale. Often, the great buys are grabbed up on the steps of the county courthouse; what's left are the ones the bank had to bid in at the sale.

It's worth noting, too, that today's home mortgage is usually a family's largest single monthly obligation. As such, it is often the first to suffer when hard times hit. In years past, a homeowner typically had substantial equity in his home and was able to sell it and stay out of the debt morass.

But, at its root, the question "How did this happen?" is, in virtually every case, actually much more difficult to answer. Who could have known that after nineteen years of marriage, a man with five children would completely disappear, leaving no way for family or friends to find him? Who could have foreseen that a man with twenty-two years on the job would decide that he was meant to be an entrepreneur—and sacrifice everything on a dubious business venture? Who can predict a plant closing, a decision to move a business to another state, sharply increased foreign competition, or any of the other factors that can suddenly make it impossible for a homeowner to meet his obligations?

Changing environments: Of banks and HUD offerings

In the mid-eighties, there were some areas of the country where realty values simply skyrocketed. In some cases, properties advanced 30 to 40 percent in a single year, an unbelievable rate. During those heady days, the properties offered at foreclosure auctions were almost guaranteed to be fought over, and fiercely. Even if a bank had to take back a property, it could rely on a broker who would help dispose of the property. Banks were never left with a large inventory of OREs. It was quite a period in the history of the industry; to some people, it looked like it would never end. It did, although the banks' mechanisms for handling foreclosed properties have remained essentially the same.

Any bank losses are alleviated by private mortgage insurance coverage, known as PMI, which is required to be taken out for mortgages in excess of 80 percent of appraised value. Today, the insurance companies are being hit hard with claims.

There is a different set of procedures with Veterans Administration and Federal Housing Administration (now referred to as Secretary Housing and Urban Development, or HUD) guaranteed loans. In these cases, the banks are out of the picture once they complete the foreclosure process. Those properties are turned over to the respective agencies once the banks acquire title; the VA and FHA have their own methods for disposing of the properties. The VA has them managed by a local broker; FHA/HUD once had a policy of fixing up the properties completely and then placing them on the market at a fair market value. That is a thing of the past, however.

At one time, I was the property management broker for FHA for southern Nassau County on Long Island, New York. The properties were brought up to excellent condition; where new kitchens, boilers, stoves, or other components were required, FHA would furnish new units. Although done by bid, the work was performed by completely competent professionals. The offerings were good values; the financing terms furnished by FHA were excellent. People buying the properties were getting a tremendous value.

In our area, the FHA had to discontinue the program and offer an all-cash, "as is" program in its stead. This is the program that is presently in effect there today. Many of the offerings are excellent values but are, unfortunately, not available for the low-cash, low-income buyer seeking affordable housing. Considering the condition of these properties, they can't be mortgaged through conventional sources. Since all cash is required, they're really open only to speculators and renovators.

Why was the "fix-up" approach halted? Consider the following story.

One Saturday morning, as I went into an advertised house to open it for public inspection, I received a big surprise as I made my way down to the basement to turn on the circuit breakers. The basement was ankle-deep in water.

Now, the plumbers had just installed a new heating system with all copper tubing throughout. And a set of enterprising thieves had entered the basement shortly afterwards and cut away all the copper tubing, presumably for resale at a junk yard.

That was outrageous, but what really made me angry was the thieves' failure to turn off the master valve. They just cut and cut—probably getting a good dousing in the process—and left the water running continuously. I had to shut off the water, resecure the property, and post a note informing visitors that the sale had been called off.

There were numerous incidents of this kind. After a while, the FHA decided that it would be less costly to sell at a lower price and avoid added expenditures that could be (and too often were) instantly wiped out by vandalism.

HUD offerings still appear in the newspapers. If you can raise the money for the unconditional purchase, it's possible to get a good buy. Offerings are by bid; the terms of the sale are listed in the ad.

Good real estate offices are familiar with the process. They can advise you and will also be able to supply the necessary

HUD forms and file them for you. The offices receive a commission from HUD, so don't feel that you're imposing on them if you seek out their help.

VA offerings

The VA sends a monthly list of its offerings to brokers who have registered with it. The VA usually does not fix up properties but offers them at a fair price.

The VA also offers very favorable financing terms, but the procedure is a bit different. It sells on an installment plan basis. You don't have an actual deed, but you do have equitable ownership. That means, in essence, that the house is yours. You can improve it and do anything to it that does not minimize the security (i.e., the home). As in a mortgage clause, you can't divest any of the property.

If you choose to sell the property at a later date for much more than you paid for it, your purchaser may arrange his financing in the ordinary way. At the closing, the VA will act in much the same way a mortgagee would. Its claim will be paid directly, and your purchaser will receive a deed from the Administrator of Veterans Affairs.

At any time after your purchase of a VA foreclosure, if you have reduced the amount of the mortgage to 75 percent of the purchase price, you receive a deed and are removed from what was actually an installment contract. (If you had paid 25 percent down at purchase you would have received a deed outright.) Until the point where the mortgage amount is reduced to 75 percent of the original purchase price, the VA is in title and the deed for your sale to a third party would have to come directly from the Administrator of Veterans Affairs.

These VA installment contracts were (and still are) an excellent source of affordable housing. Through the years, I've sold many homes by this process to persons who never believed they had sufficient cash or credit to purchase a home.

Again, your local broker should have access to these properties; he's paid a commission by the VA. Make the contact. (The only problem in higher-priced neighborhoods is that, generally speaking, there haven't been many VA loans in such areas recently, so there are no foreclosures.)

In many regions, FNMA and FMAC have appointed management brokers to help dispose of their acquisitions. Some of these brokers are members of their local Multiple Listing Service; you'll often find numerous foreclosure listings in the MLS bulletin. Your broker can access these.

For the person who needs bank financing, buying owned real estate from a bank can be the answer. If you're a credit-worthy individual, you may be pleasantly surprised to learn that the bank is actually looking for you! As I mentioned earlier, these properties represent only headaches for the bank. If you can qualify to buy, you're helping to alleviate a bad situation.

Never approach a bank with hat in hand if you're looking to purchase one of its owned properties. Believe me, if your credit history is good, it will bend over backwards to help you purchase that property.

I stated earlier that the bank can't make a profit in disposing of owned real estate. It is usually in no position to. One of the reasons the bank took the property back was that the existing obligation was greater than the price the auction-attending public was willing to spend. That's how it became an ORE!

So the bank will entertain offers. All businesspeople know that if you're going to make investments, every once in a while you're going to make a bad one. A stockholder who sees his stock plummet from 100 to 60 is often unwilling to wait until the stock reaches or exceeds its original purchase price; he may sell at 75. The bank, too, realizes its investment has taken a downturn. Accordingly, it has taken back its commodity, money, in a different form. It's now called real estate. The bank has to return the commodity to its original form (money). Getting rid of the real estate is a priority. The bank must sell.

Market forces

When you and hundreds of people are looking to purchase a given home, you must deal with the marketplace factor: competition. The price goes up if there is little or no competition for the property. However, you the buyer are in a much stronger position.

The Edsel is often referred to as one of the greatest blunders of the automobile industry, but I don't go along with that. At the time, there were low-end automobiles (Fords and Chevys) and high-end automobiles (Cadillacs and Lincolns)—and then there was the great, crowded middle market (Oldsmobiles, Buicks, Mercurys, and Chryslers). That middle segment was glutted, and it was into that group that the Edsel was marched with such fanfare. In and of itself, that might not have been such a bad decision, but the timing was bad. The country was in a serious economic recession by the time the Edsel debuted. (I remember that the industry had come up with a slogan about that time: "Help beat the recession; buy a new car.")

The real estate industry is experiencing something similar as of this writing. In the Northeast, for instance, affordable housing is below $150,000; that's where the greatest demand exists. If the property you're interested in is at that level, you won't sway the bank's officer as readily as if you were contemplating purchasing one of his Edsels. That doesn't mean you're looking for substandard housing; it does mean you stand to get a far better property if the property is one in which very few people have expressed interest.

The banks will negotiate. They want to remove the properties from their inventories. When they sell at a loss, the properties become part of their true financial picture, so a bank officer will want to work with you in such a way as to minimize the bank's loss.

That officer is much different from homeowners who must sell but are hung up on their original purchase price. Those homeowners are emotional sellers. They can point out every tack they hammered and every blade of grass they planted. Something quite personal is invested in the home. The bank officer, on the other hand, is making a business decision, and the cold logic of business does not have to contend with the many emotional distractions of the homeowner. It's a matter of dollars and cents.

The bank officer is prepared to take a loss. His only question now is. How far can he sway you without losing you?

All-cash offers

If yours is an all-cash offer, it will be far more attractive to the bank officer. With that sort of offer, there are no contingencies that can cancel the agreement. Once the bank accepts your offer and contracts to sell to you, full attention can be paid to the other troubled properties in its possession.

If you have a source for the needed cash, you present yourself as a strong, completely qualified, and very attractive potential buyer. (We'll discuss some financing arrangements that will allow you to obtain the necessary cash a little later in the book.)

Bidding

When bidding for a property, you should have a price set in your mind that is the maximum you will spend.

The bank officer handling the negotiations is usually picked for the job because he's the best "rug trader." This officer expects your initial offer to be a starting point and will treat it that way. If you offer your final price at the outset, you will have eliminated the bargaining process completely. It will be difficult to restore the sense of balance and progression good negotiating calls for. Never give the bank officer your "firm" figure at the beginning of the session.

The bank officer may make light of your initial offer. (A good many have been known to make abrasive comments at this stage, such as, "That's ridiculous.") Move up, but grudgingly.

If, when discussing the various potential prices for the property, you are asked to "split the difference," be sure that the halfway point you are being asked to accept is no greater than your predetermined price. If the figure exceeds the amount you established before beginning the negotiating process, do not agree to the terms. (You may decide to make an exception to this if the figure in question is only slightly above your predetermined price.)

If you can't get an agreement, thank the officer for considering your offer, explain that you're unable to go higher, and ask that your name be kept on file. If the property is one the bank is unlikely to get other offers on, you may get your terms then and there. If you don't, hold out. (Even if you decide to walk out the door, you may well hear from the bank at a later date.)

You should be sure to close the agreement when you and the officer arrive at the price that is acceptable to you. If you don't and the property gets away, you may have regrets later. Do be careful, though, not to "telegraph" your eagerness to purchase the property. Let the bank officer feel that you're prepared to walk away if you can't get it at your price.

Having said that, I should acknowledge that a good deal of perspective and balance is essential in negotiating, especially if you are negotiating for a property you intend to occupy yourself. No one ever moved into a "great deal." People move into homes with gardens that can be tended, workshops big enough to manage special projects, and decks that are perfect for family barbecues. If you end up paying somewhat more than some expert said you should because you know that the home is just right for you and within your financial reach, buy the property. Price will eventually be forgotten. Don't let your future be clouded by "should haves."

Opportunities

The greatest opportunities for the would-be homeowner today can probably be found in the local bank's ORE inventory.

Many banks publish their offerings in local papers each week; check them out. Make an appointment to inspect the property with the bank officer handling it. Ask questions; feel the situation out. Determine whether there have been any offers so far. If you name a price and the officer tells you that the bank turned down a higher offer a little while ago, ask if you can submit your offer in writing and have it placed in the bank's files. That way they can contact you if they have a change of heart. (Many offers come in early on in the process and are rejected in the belief that greater offers will be received; when they aren't, you can bet that the people at the bank have some second thoughts.)

Be persistent. If you don't hear from the bank, call. You may be able to reach a compromise figure that furthers everyone's interests.

CHAPTER FIVE

Deed in Lieu of Foreclosure

There may be among you readers someone who is not necessarily looking to buy a foreclosed property but is contemplating the effect of foreclosure.

What do I mean by that? Well, at all times we have people who are changing employment and in need of a move to another locality, maybe many states away.

In the case of company transfers, there is usually no problem. The company will buy the home at a predetermined figure. The company will then continue the sale and will be responsible for the care in the event of vacancy. Not all job moves are within the company. Sometimes the transferor is doing it on his own. He has been offered a better position elsewhere, but the responsibility of the move is completely his. First of the items to be completed is the sale of his present domicile. It is possible that he had anticipated an out of town move sometime before and had put his home up for sale. Now several months later, he finds that a sale at the figure he wants is out of sight. Nothing in the neighborhood is moving. The price he is being offered would not even cover his mortgage. In addition, he would have to pay a brokerage fee. This would force him to dip into his small savings he had hoped would cover the transfer.

Looks hopeless, doesn't it? What should he do? Call in a mover and drift into the night and let the bank foreclose?

That could be a solution, but as the bank notices pile up and the foreclosure commences, what happens to his usually impeccable credit history? Not a particularly good solution, is it?

Well, how about renting it out? That could be a solution. But what if your good tenant loses his job or gets sick and cannot make his rent payments? This happens.

You see, on the whole, renters are generally people who do not have the wherewithal to purchase a home, and so they rent. Their credit patterns are not as secure as those of homeowners. Well, there you are in Colorado and your bank back in New Jersey wants its mortgage payments.

That's just one scenario. There are so many things that can happen.

You did not buy the house to rent it out. You bought it to live in. At this point your equity is very little or nil. Your credit has been good, you have paid all your bills, and there are no judgments or legal proceedings pending against you. If you walk away from the mortgage and leave the path open to the bank to commence the foreclosure proceeding against you, you have given it a burden. The burden is the foreclosure procedure, which requires time and money. In addition, the bank now has an empty house that it must protect. If it does not, the house could be stripped and vandalized, resulting in untold repairs and replacements.

Under these circumstances, you could offer the bank a deed in lieu of foreclosure. What is that?

You go up to your banker and tell him that you are leaving the state and that you have attempted to sell the house and have been unable to do so and are offering the bank title to the house "as is" and you want to go on your way.

Well, the bank is not required to accept a deed from you, but what are the alternatives if it does not? Either way, it is going to have an empty house to add to its inventory with all of the problems that attend such circumstances.

In the event of the foreclosure proceeding, if the bank gets a call from an interested buyer, what can it do? It would have to tell him to wait until it completes the legal process. Now the process can take months and even years.

The former owner has to be served with court papers. If the bank does not know where he is, this may have to be done by publication. This means further delays and expense. All this can be avoided by acceptance of the deed from the mortgagor, you.

So, when you approach the banker to accept a deed, he is going to ask you about your credit. Are there any liens against the property? The bank will conduct a search of all the public records, and if it is clean it will gladly accept a deed.

This brings me to the purpose of my introducing this process in a book on foreclosures. After all, the property was not foreclosed, but now it is a part of the bank's OREs.

Now the bank is in the position of the former owner. It has a property to sell. It has to get rid of it. The property has to be reduced to money, the commodity of bank commerce. It does not make the bank's balance sheet look better. Owned Real Estate (ORE) or, as some banks show, REO (Real Estate Owned), is not an asset. It is a liability. In this position, this real estate is like the bonds you bought for $1,000, which you now want to sell. You discover that bank rates have risen above the interest you are receiving and you now have to sell at a discount. The banks are used to this concept. They have no trouble in adjusting to the market conditions and they will sell the property for less than the mortgage balance.

You could not have gotten this deal from the former home-owner. He could not do it. But the bank can do it and does do it. That is why I advise all persons who are looking to buy fore-closures to contact the banks first. The best opportunities for a great buy are from the bank's inventory.

As I state, have stated, and will continue to state, if you are credit worthy, the bank will be very happy to deal with you and you might get a very favorable mortgage loan from it as well.

I would like to tell you of a case that happened to a dear friend of mine. She had seen a house with a broker in a very fine area of Westchester County, New York. The house was owned by one of the New York banks. It was very impressively perched on a promontory and had commanding views on all sides. The bank was asking $185,000. Although the house was in good shape, the prior owner had started several improvements that were not yet completed and these involved plumbing and elec-trical work. The work that had been done was all of excellent quality. I advised her to offer $100,000, all cash. The bank agreed to accept $120,000. I arranged a source for interim financing for her and then secured a mortgage loan for $135,000. The $15,000 excess plus the $10,000 she had was more than enough to cover the repairs plus closing costs.

Shortly after she moved in, she had a call from the village clerk. The clerk asked, "Did you pay only $120,000 for that house?" When told yes, the clerk continued, "We have it appraised for $314,000."

Now I am not telling you that you can duplicate this. I would just like to impress upon you to check the banks. There are still plenty of good deals to be bought directly from the banks.

At the foreclosure sale, you do not know what is in the house. When the bank owns it, you can get in and check it out. If you want to bring a plumber friend or an engineer, you will have access and will be able to gauge your costs.

Homes taken by deeds in lieu of foreclosure are probably the better homes in the banks' inventory because the former owners did not lose the home. They probably took excellent care until they moved.

When you were out shopping for a home, you may have made an offer on a house and were told, "Your price is lower than my mortgage. I would sooner turn it over to the bank." When you hear that, this home is now owned by the bank; go see the bank officer and make a deal. You may very well get it for the figure you set previously.

CHAPTER SIX

Other Reasons for Foreclosure

Occasionally, you may read in your local paper about public sale of tax liens. Taxes take precedence over all other claims—including those of the mortgage.

Some background on this type of foreclosure is probably in order. Prior to World War II, the banks took payments of principal and interest only; mortgagors were permitted to make tax payments directly to the receiver of taxes. One of the main considerations in allowing this was the fact that the ratio of debt to value in those days was usually quite low. If the bank had to foreclose and pay up back taxes, the value of the property was sufficient to cover all obligations.

With the advent of the Federal Housing Administration and the provisions of the Servicemen's Readjustment Act of 1944, however, low equity mortgage situations became more common. The Veterans Administration permitted homes to be bought for no cash down, that is, the VA guaranteed 100 percent of the mortgage. The FHA administered a low-cash down payment program for nonveterans, requiring as little as 3 percent down payment.

Banks became concerned about the prospect of purchasers failing to make tax and insurance payments when due. Under existing arrangements, taxing authorities could have taken over the property in such cases, mortgage or no mortgage. To correct this, trust fund arrangements were set up with lenders.

These new mortgage arrangements provided that payments for taxes and insurance would be prepaid to the mortgagee, who would then pay the obligation when due. It was a fine setup that brought a measure of discipline to the process, and the same procedure was eventually transferred to conventional bank practices.

Today, most mortgagees require that escrow funds be established with the bank for the purpose of making sure that taxes are paid on time and that fire insurance is continually in force. The funds can provide another source of bank money; although they are escrow or trust funds, in some jurisdictions they may be used by the bank in normal banking practices. Most banks, of course, are regulated by state laws. Some states require that a percentage of the total amount be maintained and do not restrict the movement of the unregulated portion.

The majority of banks calculate the amount of the escrow based upon a need factor, although some build in large cushions in these accounts. Because of this practice, many states require that interest be paid on the escrow accounts since they are savings reserves and belong to the borrower. The amount of interest is usually a token figure, often as little as 2 percent a year.

As we have seen, banks want to do business with you, the borrower. That point should be even clearer to you when you realize how the bank benefits from escrow balances. Add in all the various servicing fees, and you can readily see that banks do well when they loan out money at favorable interest rates to persons with good credit.

Tax sales

Most tax sales don't originate with properties that are mortgaged with regulated mortgage companies or banks. They take place on properties that are usually free and clear of mortgages.

That this is so is not difficult to understand, given the elaborate safeguards just discussed. Payment of taxes is a vital part of the bank's mortgage procedures. It is quite rare for a regulated lender to neglect to pay taxes. In fact, in today's computerized society, it's almost *impossible* to forget to pay taxes due on mortgage accounts.

Who, then, defaults because of problems with tax payments? In many cases, senior citizens who simply don't understand their obligations; no one tells them about what payments must be made or the consequences of nonpayment.

Often, a husband dies and the widow is completely unable to cope with taking care of what she regards as business pursuits. A summons arrives in the mail; she ignores it. A judgment is made against her; she doesn't understand it. Someone buys the lien; she doesn't know about it. The legal machinery cranks onward slowly; she assumes things have blown over. She is usually the last person to learn that she no longer owns the property. Sadly, there was no one in her circle to make clear to her the gravity of her situation.

In such an unfortunate (but not uncommon) case, the system progresses regardless of the state of knowledge of the homeowner. Tax sales and foreclosure actions are instituted. These sales (and sheriff's sales, which we'll examine a little later) differ from the foreclosure sale in that there are often homestead exemptions and redemption periods involved.

Let's look at the mechanics of the tax sale. When the municipality puts the tax liens up for sale, that taxing authority (usually the county) is selling the bid to the public. Depending on local statute, the party who buys the claim has the right to claim title to the property after expiration of the statutory time for redemption. That period could be perhaps one or two years, depending on local law.

During the redemption period, interest is accruing at a rate permitted under the statute. This rate could be as much as 20 percent. You can see, then, that the person who purchases tax liens has a good deal. He is offered a good rate of return on his investment, and if the defaulting party does not redeem the lien, then he has acquired a good property at very little cost.

Sheriff's sales

Recovery by a creditor for obligations other than mortgage default is usually carried out by means of a sheriff's sale. In these actions there are other considerations and regulations that enter into the process. I must stress here once again that there is no national law on these subjects; they are governed by local law. You should consult your lawyer with respect to any of these situations.

Many states and municipalities have homestead exemptions, which apply in sheriff's sales for judgments other than mortgage debt. The exemption is usually expressed in dollar amounts. New York, for instance, has a $10,000 exemption. What this means is that if you acquire a property under this type of sale, you must give an allowance of $10,000 to the foreclosed party.

Why is such a measure necessary? There were once some pretty shady characters who abused the system, buying up judgments from creditors and foreclosing mercilessly on unfortunate owners. The homestead exemption is one small window of protection for the homeowner. Without it, many victimized homeowners (particularly widows) would be destitute.

In addition, you should know that foreclosure actions by sheriff's sale differ from customary mortgage foreclosures in that they usually carry with them a right of redemption. The period in which the defaulting party has the opportunity to make restitution is generally identified by local statute. Such a provision constitutes another protection for the person in default.

Nonmonetary reasons for default

Foreclosure actions can be instituted for nonmonetary reasons, too, although this is surprising to many people. The trick is to remember that the mortgage agreement is a contract; when you breach a contract, there are avenues of relief open to the aggrieved party. You can't rewrite what you agreed to according to what you believe it should be. If you break the agreement, you may well face some unpleasant consequences.

Today one of the most common nonmonetary reasons for default is the sale to a third party of property subject to an existing mortgage that is nonassumable and "due on sale." That means that in the event of a transfer, the mortgage must be paid up. The remedy for breach is foreclosure.

There are other reasons for nonmonetary actions, including breach of covenants and restrictions contained in the mortgage and divestment of any part of the mortgaged security, whether it be land or appurtenances—buildings attached to the property. When these conditions exist, the mortgagee has the right to accelerate the payments, in other words, call for payment of the entire principal balance, even though all the monthly payments have been made. In these instances, the payment history is not at issue; the nonmonetary violations are of such a nature that the mortgagee wants out. The option of making payments on a monthly basis is simply revoked.

Third-party actions

Occasionally a foreclosure action will be halted before the sale by the action of a third party who pays the plaintiff (the mortgagee) and takes an assignment of the proceeding. One of the most common reasons for this is that the new successor mortgagee has considerable obligations due him and is seeking to protect his interest by controlling the foreclosure. By getting an assignment of the foreclosure action, the third party can protect his interest and acquire the title without the penalty of the other liens. (His interest may be by mortgage or judgment, of course.) Such a lien is a junior lien to others; if the foreclosure sale is not carried out, the initial liens still apply to the property.

I had an experience with an interesting case that shows how this works. It involved a divorced couple; the wife continued to live in the house and was quite content there, but the husband had stopped making the mortgage payments. The wife, wishing to avoid making any payments that would enrich the husband, also failed to pay the bank. A foreclosure action resulted.

The wife's brother, an attorney, wanted to ensure that his sister could continue living in her home. He purchased the mortgage from the bank and continued the action. (A puzzling choice; one might have expected him to simply stop at that point, but read on.)

The auction was duly scheduled; the brother entered as a bidder, determined to overcome all others trying to obtain the property. This he did, and once he owned the house outright he allowed his sister to remain there permanently. He was willing to bid well above market value because he would become the owner; any excess sums that were bid would inure to his sister's benefit. (Of course, the husband had an interest in any surplus money received; presumably the attorney/brother made the proper arrangements with him.) The end result? The initial squabble had been resolved, the brother prevailed, and his sister remained in the house.

Now don't get the idea that you can divest an ex-spouse of interest in a jointly owned home by buying up the mortgage and foreclosing. There is a little warning you should bear in mind before you embark on such a course of action.

It is a criminal act to purchase a mortgage for the sole purpose of foreclosing.

How, then, did the brother get away with his purchase? Remember: The foreclosure action had been started by the bank. The brother stepped in to protect his sister; he did not initiate the proceeding.

CHAPTER SEVEN

Before the Sale

Broadly speaking, there are three types of people who look to purchase foreclosures.

The first group is made up of those who are seeking to buy a home to live in and are attracted to foreclosures because they are affordable. I call them "nesters."

The second group comprises people who already have a place to live but would change it if they could get a good buy in some area that represents upward mobility to them. I call this group the "climbers."

The third group is made up of individuals who want to buy for rental income and/or future appreciation. I would include in this group real estate professionals looking to buy low and sell high. I call these people "pros."

The nesters

Many of the people in this group have almost no cash, little in the way of established credit, and employment records that are still developing. No- and low-cash down arrangements with 30 year mortgages may have worked 30 years ago for first-time homebuyers, but these conditions don't exist today on properties that are being offered for public auction.

The typical basis for these auction sales is 10 percent of the price with the opening bid; the balance is due *in cash* within 30 days. That's a tall order for a young couple with one or two children still trying to make ends meet.

Often, there is a belief that "the bank will loan the balance" after the 10 percent deposit is managed. This assumption ignores the fact that a sold property has many problems the ordinary property being foreclosed does not have, including (but not limited to) difficulties with accessibility, ability to pass inspection, terminated utility services, hostile occupants, and general physical appearance.

Many people reading this book will qualify as nesters. If the advice on bidding and auctions that follows in this chapter is unworkable for you, take a hint. Set your sights on the bank's OREs. Don't go the auction route only to learn that the commitment you've made will not be supported by any bank in your area. As we have seen, the banks will give you generous terms on something they cannot unload in any other way if they think you can afford the property. You may not get the once-in-a-lifetime deal you'd hoped to come across at the foreclosure sale, but then again...

The climbers

Those attempting to benefit from defaults in high-income areas are often unsuccessful. Foreclosures that take place in these neighborhoods are typically too expensive for the climbers—auction or no auction. The climber's best bet is to wait out the foreclosure sale, or even attend it to see if the property ends up with the bank as the new owner.

The pros

Professionals are common attendees at foreclosure sales. These people, who do not usually have problems coming up with the funds to secure property, can be quite formidable competitors.

If you are a bidder for investment, you will eventually find yourself in competition with members of this group. If they feel you are a novice, there is a good chance that they will try to hurt you by bidding you up to pay a price that will prove to be a bad investment. They want to eliminate you as a future competitor.

The professionals know each other and work within a loose network. This is not to suggest that they are noncompetitive. Although they don't actually get together before sales to set limits, they may have a general feel for whose "turn" it is to get the best of a deal.

You have to be pretty strong to buck them, but if you're prepared, you can protect yourself. (You can, for instance, pull out and leave an aggressive professional holding a bid that's too high. He'll soon reconsider your status as a novice.)

Financing

Regardless of your circumstances, if you are trying to secure a piece of property at auction you will need to make arrangements so that you'll have the bid money immediately and the balance in cash in 30 days.

Consider a home equity loan; it's one of the very best options open to you. If you own a home, you will learn—if you don't already know—that banks are competing to loan you money on what is basically a second mortgage on your present home. (Of course, if you have no existing mortgage, the new one can't be a second mortgage.) As a rule of thumb, the bank will loan you up to 75 percent of the appraised value less any existing mortgage.

You don't have to borrow the money immediately. You can go through the entire procedure, get a commitment for the total sum, and take out the cash only when you want to use it. The arrangement is similar to a business's line of credit at the bank. You can take cash as needed and pay interest only each month on the unpaid balance. There are no monthly repayment commitments, but if you choose to reduce at any time your next monthly interest payment is reduced.

You'll be required to pay interest only. If you have reduced the principal balance and find a future need for funds, you can again borrow up to the original 75 percent figure. There is no requirement to pay it up for five years. At the end of the five-year period, the loan will become a permanent loan and you will then be required to retire it on a 15 year amortization basis.

If you're an investor, you can use any part of the money, when and if you need it. Let's say you use it to purchase and fix up property. You can then apply for a permanent mortgage loan on the new property and pay off the equity loan.

Or say you're a young couple seeking affordable housing. You may be able to get one of the sets of parents to make the home equity commitment and loan you the necessary funds. When you're in title, you can apply for a permanent mortgage. There's just one caution in order: If you're in title, the loan is actually a refinance. On a conventional mortgage refinance, the bank will usually give only up to 75 percent of the appraised value of the home. The procedure is different from that followed in a first-time purchase.

Suppose that 75 percent figure falls short of what you owe; there are a couple of avenues you can follow. The first is to purchase the home in your parents' names. They can then contract to sell it to you, and as a purchaser you can get as much as a 95 percent loan. You can then get sufficient cash to pay not only for the purchase, but for the needed repairs as well. (If you're within FHA guidelines, you might even get more favorable terms. Consult a good local mortgage broker.)

When you have your permanent loan you can pay the parents back for the down payment, interest, and costs involved; they can repay the home equity loan. All you'll owe is heartfelt gratitude, and in all likelihood, the parents will be overjoyed to have helped you bring it all about. Everyone will be happy: you'll have encountered one of life's win-win situations.

Of course, not all of us are in a position to take advantage of such an arrangement. Let's talk now about "hard money" lenders. As we learned earlier in the book, the greater the risk, the greater the return must be. There are places you can contact ahead of time that will be a fairly good bet to give you the commitment you need, but you must remember that this is not an easy situation. You're seeking to purchase a property that's coming up for sale. You haven't bid yet. There's no certainty that yours will be the winning bid, and there's no guarantee what that bid amount will be.

These are not insurmountable problems, but you may have to spend some money on inspections, despite the fact that the property may never be yours. Other than that, the question boils down to one of interest. You give the lender your credit information in advance; if all checks out, you learn how much you could borrow. That commitment is based on your credit (although the lender may not make all the money available to you if the property is somehow questionable). The point is, though, that the money the lender advances is *not* long term; as a result, it's at a higher rate than the customary bank mortgage. Charges are often more, too.

Before you get angry, stop and think. The lender is making it possible for you to buy a $100,000 house for $50,000. His rate, probably about 16 percent, is higher than that charged by the banks—but the banks won't take this kind of risk! The reason for the short term on the mortgage is that you're expected to go out for a permanent loan once you've acquired title and made the improvements. So don't be horrified; say "thank you"! At least your interest payments lessen as you pay. (The same can't be said for most credit cards, which charge similar rates and compound interest charges.)

In business, manufacturers borrow from hard money lenders (or "factors") on a continuous basis and are happy to get the loans. They help the companies stay in business, and the borrowers know it. Hard money lenders, if used properly, can make some pretty impossible-sounding dreams come true.

Lawyers and the sale

People often ask whether they should take a lawyer with them to the sale. The answer is probably no. There's little or nothing a lawyer will be able to do for you at the sale itself. The terms are published; they won't be altered. Although I believe in using lawyers in all real estate transactions, the only thing they can do with regard to a foreclosure is order title insurance. You probably won't need a lawyer for that; usually, the company that did the bank's search will be glad to give you a title policy at standard rates.

An explanation of a title policy is in order here. You can order an "abstract of title," which is a search of title, but it will not insure you. Such an abstract merely checks the records.

The policy that insures your interest is called by different names depending on what part of the country you're from. "Title policy" and "fee policy" are the most common. If you get a mortgage from a lender at the time you purchase the property, you will also pay for a mortgage policy for the bank. That insures the bank against something going wrong with the property's established and accepted chain of ownership. Over and above that amount, you should arrange to pay a lesser figure to insure your own interests as well.

In essence, you are insuring your ownership. If any person or organization materializes with a valid claim to the property that overrides yours, the title company makes good. Such coverage is an absolute necessity in a foreclosure purchase. Check with your local agent to get information on the varieties of coverage available.

In my forty-plus years of experience, I've personally seen only one claim that could affect the total value of a property. You will find that other professionals in the real estate field have similar experience with this issue. Such problems are extremely rare.

Engineer's reports

These days, if you engage the services of a young lawyer, you're likely to be advised to "get an engineer's report" on the property before signing anything. This has more to do with the C.Y.A. (cover your anatomy) training they give lawyers today than with any tangible benefit to you. If he advises you in this way, the lawyer is essentially inoculating himself against any problems that may eventually come up with the property. You may be interested to learn that for the first twenty-five of my years in the real estate business, no one had ever heard of an engineer's report. People looked houses over and bought them. I never heard anyone complain of buying a "pig in a poke."

Today's lawyers, though, will advise you to get the report *before* you buy the house. This means that if you don't win with your bid, or if you run into some snag that has nothing to do with the report (and these are not exactly uncommon developments) you will have paid $300 to inspect a property you will never own. Moreover, the defaulting mortgagors or tenants are in possession of the building. What do you think are the chances they won't let the engineer in? What do you think are the chances you'll be charged for his time anyway?

If you want to have an engineer check the house *after* you've bought it, by all means do so. But ask yourself what he's going to tell you. That the plumbing leaks? That the oil burner is shot? That the electrical system needs to be upgraded? Are these things you wouldn't deduce on your own? You've just purchased a foreclosed house. You know it may need some work. That $300 fee will pay a good portion of the plumber's bill. And the oil company will check your heating system and tell you what repairs are needed; after he fixes it, the repairman will give you a service contract. There are a lot of good electricians out there who can check the wiring for you and do what's necessary for you. They may not be able to turn out a fancy report, though.

These are my opinions, of course; the final choice is yours. But you should know there is a distinct possibility that the real reasons the engineer's report is recommended have as much to do with the lawyer's peace of mind as with yours. Think twice before acquiescing.

Inspecting vacant properties

It is not uncommon for the property being foreclosed to be vacant. The mortgagors abandon the property; perhaps a neighbor notifies the bank out of concern that vandals may torch the property and put other homes in danger.

The bank sends a crew out to board up the house and secure it, although it does not own the property at this point. It is merely taking steps to protect an investment. No one wants to see the home become the target of neighborhood kids or a domicile for transients.

It may be possible to contact the bank and arrange for an inspection of such a property. Obviously, there are significant risks in taking on an abandoned house; in this case, you should definitely attempt to get a look at the property before you make any commitment. If you can, get a general contractor to accompany you on the visit. You may be able to get a good idea of the amount of work involved in this way.

One largely overlooked factor that is not a matter of public record has to do with environmental and zoning problems. Such difficulties are showing up with greater and greater frequency these days and may very well be the reason the mortgagor walked away from the property.

You're probably already familiar with the horror stories about radon, asbestos removal, gasoline contamination from nearby storage tanks, and the like. Do a little creative research; make sure you're not walking into a nightmare.

Some years ago, a fellow offered me a very attractive property at what seemed like a remarkably low price. I did some research and learned that the deal that seemed to be too good to be true really was. A trip to the state Department of Transportation yielded the information that a proposed roadway was slated to pass right through the house. I politely declined the offer.

The possibility exists that the property you have your eye on breaches local zoning laws. These violations will have to be corrected before you complete the deal, and they might be costly. Don't wait for the title company to tell you that the two-family house you bought is zoned as a one-family house. Once the title company gets into the act, you've already put a bid in! Take a trip to the town's building department and confirm that you are looking at a legal two-family unit. Do this before the sale.

It may be possible that you are looking at a two-family house in an area that is zoned for one family. You may have a situation here that precedes the date of the zoning laws and is permitted because certificates of occupancy for two-family houses weren't issued at that time.

In this case, if you are planning to use the income from the rental apartment in your credit statement, it's possible that the bank may not accept it. In the event of a fire or wind damage, the town would not permit you to restore it as a two-family. The new construction must conform to the present zoning restrictions. When you buy this type of property, you are taking that risk.

Junior lienors

Others besides the bank that issued the first mortgage may have an interest in the property; be prepared to encounter junior lienors at the sale if the existing mortgage is low. You can expect them to bid the price up to a level that will cover their interests, even if they have to buy the property themselves. Chances are, though, that they won't want to buy it—they'll simply want their money. As a very rough guideline, then, you can expect to pay a sum equal to the first mortgage plus the second mortgage for the property.

Don't let the fact that a second mortgage shows up in the Lis Pendens keep you away. There's no guarantee that second lienors will be at the sale. Occasionally they will have been paid off, but the transaction will have gone unrecorded due to an error on the part of the mortgagor, leaving the second mortgage on record. There is only way to be absolutely certain: Attend the sale.

CHAPTER EIGHT

The Sale

Foreclosure sales can be held just about anywhere that is centrally located and accessible. They are typically held on the courthouse steps (weather permitting) or in Town Hall. By the way, when the notice refers to the courthouse steps, it really does mean the steps outside the building. If you're in any doubt as to whether the front or rear steps are being used, ask a receptionist or guard for directions.

Be early. It is often far too late to arrive at 9:03 for a sale that is scheduled for 9 A.M. sharp. Don't take the chance that the parade will pass you by; show up well before the appointed time. (The day before the sale is scheduled you should call the office of the attorney who has been appointed receiver to confirm that it is still on.)

Chances are that you won't be alone on the steps. You've thought the property worthy of consideration, and you can expect others to, as well. The sale will begin with a recital of the action by the referee; we'll learn more about this person a little later. After this introduction is concluded, the referee begins the sale. This may be over in as little as three minutes. You can see now why promptness is so essential

Buying from the winning bidder

We've discussed the "pros" a little earlier, those regulars who purchase properties, fix them up, and then offer them for sale. I can tell you something about these bidders: They know their markets. What's more, they know what to expect once they've purchased the property. They know how to cope with problems.

They are not buying the property to live in, however. And that may be a very important piece of information for you.

If yours is not the winning bid (or if you choose not to bid at all because of cash constraints), you can speak to the winner at the sale site and make a commitment to buy it from him, then and there. You'll be saving him money. All he's putting out at that time is the 10 percent down payment. He'll have a very short holding period while you're getting your financing and he can pass the savings on to you. Under these circumstances you can make a highly favorable transaction. The winning bidder is often happy to give you the time to secure permanent financing—and you may be able to get valuable information from this person on the best sources for mortgage money, as well.

The reason I'm suggesting that you speak to these people is that they usually offer their properties at a far more competitive price than the rest of the market. They know what is moving and for how much; they tend to price their properties below that level. What's more, they are eager to find buyers quickly; holding properties for a long time dissipates profit potential. Unlike homeowners who are emotionally tied to the homes they've lived in, these operators do not fall in love with the merchandise. They are engaged in a business venture. If you can help them turn a quick profit, they'll be amenable to your purchase offer.

Don't latch on to the first professional you meet; make the effort to get to know a few of them. Some of these folks are knowledgeable, reasonable businesspeople; others would tear the wings off butterflies for relaxation. Let the buyer beware. Reduce all agreements to writing, no matter how charming your contact is. Show everything to your attorney before signing.

Properties to avoid

The opening bid price at the auction is called the "upset price." This price is determined by the amount due the bank, which would include the mortgage balance, all charges for late payments, plus costs incurred in the foreclosure action such as legal charges, title charges, process service, publication, and other expenses. Add it all together and you have the amount that is due the bank. At the sale, the bid is usually opened by a representative of the bank. This person makes the opening bid in the event no one else does. That bid of the bank's will be the upset price.

I said the bid is *usually* opened by a representative of the bank. Occasionally, though, a mortgagee will not bid in at the sale. It hardly seems logical that someone who is owed money secured by real property would refuse to bid on the property. What underlies such a strategy?

The answer lies in the fact that, as a creditor, the mortgagee is not charged with the responsibilities of ownership. If the bank knows there are building or health code violations or derelict automobiles strewn about the front yard that must be disposed of, for example, it may not bid on the property in question. As long as the bank is not in title, it's just another aggrieved party. Once the bank becomes the owner, it has all the responsibilities of ownership. If there are no counterbalancing advantages from the bank's point of view, there may be no bid, and, assuming no one else wants the property, it may end up with the taxing authorities.

The lesson for you? If you do not hear a bid from the bank to start things off, beware. They may know something you don't.

Consider a typical area reflecting these conditions: uptown Manhattan. Here, rent controls prevented real estate operators from getting a fair return on their properties. The controls had their roots in the wartime emergency housing measures of the 1940s, but eventually became a political football. People with no business knowledge set standards for the rental industry that were so low and so onerous that landlords, realizing they were losing money by holding on to their properties, just gave up in the same way the bank gave up in the example above. Eventually, people will stop spending good money for bad results and walk away. In such cases, urban renewal projects are the most likely result, and public authorities will propose their solutions for the stricken areas.

And stricken is exactly the word for what you'll find here. If you've ever spent any time in New York City, you know that Manhattan has many such areas (as do Brooklyn and the Bronx). As you drive through these parts of the city, you might think you're taking a tour of Berlin shortly after the Allied victory in World War II. Gutted, boarded-up buildings are everywhere; the region is not a neighborhood at all but a permanent disaster area. Unless you have access to an unlimited amount of capital funds, don't ever bid for these properties.

Postponements

Last-minute postponement of the sale is not uncommon. Often, the action will be resolved or postponed at the eleventh hour, and the receiver will appear on the steps to express his apologies to all those who showed up for the sale. Of course, these plans can be changed again. If you're interested in the property, keep in touch with the receiver; sometimes the only thing holding up the sale is a legal technicality that must be attended to.

Who gets the money?

As we have seen, banks are not out to foreclose your property and then sell it off at a profit. The bank can only make a claim for the amount of its judgment. That is usually the amount of the upset price; the overage is known as "surplus money."

Surplus money is paid out to the junior lien holders in the order of the priority of their liens. This is not an automatic process. A junior lien holder who knows that the property was sold for a price in excess of the upset price can't simply sit back and wait for a check; There is a process known as a surplus money proceeding in which the junior lien holder makes an application to the receiver, through the court, for the claim. It's the obligation of the junior lien holder to make claim and certify that the debt in question was never repaid.

Other costs

We've established that costs are incurred in the pursuance of a foreclosure action and that these costs become part of the process by being included in the upset price. What other costs will the purchaser at auction have?

Well, virtually none if you want to live like a Mississippi riverboat gambler. There are some outlays you should make, however, to protect yourself, and chief among these is a title policy. We've discussed this briefly earlier in the book. Essentially, title insurance is your protection against someone challenging your right to own the property. If you've managed to find a lender to fund your purchase, that lender will require a mortgage policy, but this will not protect you. It will only protect the lending institution. Cover yourself as well.

Suppose you've paid someone to do a title search and it's come up clean; there is no record of any snag in the chain of ownership of the property. The coast appears to be clear. No one seems to have any grounds to challenge your title. Why should you pay extra for title insurance when you're already in possession of all the facts and have found nothing to worry about?

There's only one reason, but it's a compelling one that overrides everything. You pay to protect yourself against what *hasn't* shown up in the record and could come forth and be a valid, sustainable objection to title. It is true that these claims are quite rare, but some of the reasons that have surfaced have been so far-fetched as to seem inconceivable. But it could happen to you, and even an illegitimate claim has to be defended. That costs money. If you don't have insurance, you'll have to pay it out of your own pocket.

If you *do* get the insurance, however, the title company will send its lawyers to represent you no matter what the claim is, just as in an auto accident case. If you're found to be at fault, the company will pay any award.

No one will require you to buy title insurance. But if you don't want to, I recommend that you don't buy real estate, either. Too many titles have been clouded by missing heirs, creditors, forged documents, and who knows what else to take the risk.

The only other charge you'll need to consider is that of recording your deed. Again, this is not required. But if you fail to record the deed the public has no notice that the property has been transferred. You've just purchased a property that had a previous owner who was in all kinds of financial hot water. If you don't record your deed and put an end to his ownership as far as the public is concerned, you may find that a few more unwelcome claims against the property have materialized. This is not the time to pinch pennies. Your best course is to record the deed in the customary manner. *(Note:* If you choose to buy title insurance, you don't have the option of not paying to record the deed; the title company will see that this takes place.)

A little more background is probably in order about title insurance. In a foreclosure judgment, the court appoints a receiver to conduct the sale. This receiver is called a referee and has the power to sell the property and to sign a valid, legally acceptable deed (known as a "referee's deed"). When the referee signs that deed, any interest of the previous owner is terminated. The new owners have title, but not necessarily good title.

Most deeds contain covenants, warranties, and agreements that are passed along with the deed. A referee's deed doesn't contain any such covenants and warranties; it gives you title, period. If the bank's title company uncovered any zoning or occupancy violations, the company is not obligated. Their job is to give you marketable title; they insure your *ownership* of the property, although not your *right to occupy* it as it exists. The title company is giving you what it got, and nothing more. You can't even look to the bank for redress, because you didn't really buy the property from the bank. (In fact, you were in competition with it.)

We saw a little earlier how there is always the potential for zoning or building code violations. These are excepted by the title company. "Excepted" means that the company is not insuring the items in question, and that you cannot look to the company for correction of the problems. When the title closer tells you that he is excepting something, make sure you understand what he is talking about! Ask questions. Exceptions on your title policy don't mean that you won't get marketable title. They are simply the title company's way of disclaiming responsibility for problems that may arise in certain narrow areas.

Congratulations!

You are now the proud owner of a foreclosed property— warts and all. What next?

CHAPTER NINE

After the Sale

You now own a foreclosed property. In other types of real estate transactions, you usually sit down with the prior owner and work out a date of possession. These types of meetings sometimes go well, but sometimes they result in bitter conflicts and even cancellation of the agreement to sell. Here you have no agreement for possession; what's more, you're faced with hostile people in possession of what is now rightfully yours. You have to get them out. This is a sobering notion. You may well find yourself encountering emotional obstacles you hadn't counted on.

I'm not a lawyer, so I'm not going to advise you on the ins and outs of getting the people out in your area. I can forward two cautionary notes. First, your right to get the current occupants out may be limited or curtailed in a rent-controlled area. (This status may or may not have been revealed in the court papers.) Second, if you do plan to resort to legal action to take possession of the property, do yourself a favor and get a lawyer who knows the process. Find someone with experience in landlord-tenant claims. Remember that even a lawyer who specializes in real estate contracts may not know the proper procedure for removing unwanted tenants. And that's what the former owner is now.

How do you find the best lawyer for the job? Ask the clerk of the court for leads. Such attorneys appear before him on a regular basis. The lawyer you're likely to end up with through this route is probably not going to give you any problems when it comes to spending the required amount of time in court. There are probably six other cases that he needs to try at the same time.

Don't ask your college roommate, the corporate attorney, to handle the job for you. You will regret such a choice and probably spend far too much money. You won't give offense; your old roommate knows he's not a specialist in this area. He'd probably rather focus on his own practice anyway.

Surprise, surprise

People often resent moving out of a foreclosed property. Sometimes they express their resentment in strange ways.

I can't begin to tell you some of the things former owners have done to property. If I did, this book would probably earn an X rating. Let's just say that former owners can perform outrageous acts of vandalism.

There is a way to mitigate this, however. One of the simultaneous acts of home ownership is securing a fire policy. The moment you take title, you own the home; you should be prepared with insurance coverage. You can get extended coverage on your policy to cover vandalism and malicious mischief, which, it should be noted, can happen even if the prior owners moved out without incident. You may have to show the property to someone else—a lender, for instance. You won't want to conduct a tour of a vandalized home, so be sure to look things over beforehand and make whatever repairs are necessary. If you can't do it yourself, consider getting a legitimate estimate from a contractor. You can submit this to the lender you want to get a permanent mortgage loan from, then set up a schedule for the repairs to be made and the property to be reinspected. Just about any disagreement of this sort can be reduced to a question of money. (This goes for many, many problems in the real estate field!) Your lender may feel the situation is impossible, but if you have done your homework you can usually find a solution that is acceptable to both of you.

Although a mortgage with a hard money lender calls for a short-term loan, you should ask for the right to pay it off sooner. If you have this right, you may be able to place your permanent mortgage sooner and reduce the interest factor. Of course, it's possible that your hard money lender wants the loan to go to full term because he is counting on the investment return. That's his prerogative. Remember, this lender provides an essential service and is entitled to certain considerations.

Full-term mortgages

Now you're prepared to go for your full-term permanent mortgage. As we have noted, you are now refinancing; you're already an owner and are seeking a substitute mortgage, which will be a loan from the conventional sources.

Perhaps you are a first-time home buyer. You've heard that your state permits lower-rate, highly advantaged mortgages to first-time buyers. Unfortunately, you can't qualify—yours is not a purchase money mortgage, but a refinance. If availing yourself of these state mortgages is part of your planning, you would do well to plan to buy at the auction in someone else's name, as outlined in an earlier chapter.

When it comes to the amount you'll have to borrow, the bank's appraisal is all-important. This appraisal will have nothing to do with the price you paid for the property. The appraiser inspects the property, and the resulting valuation is based on what comparable properties are selling for. This means completed sales—not what someone you know has been asking for a house for the last two years.

Banks like to look at comparable sales within the last six months. Markets change rapidly today; a few years ago, one could expect comparable sales to trail behind the market by much longer than half a year, but no more. These days, a market can decline so dramatically that a sale of eight months ago could now be completely overpriced.

Appraisers could be a little less conservative in days gone by because even if they were a bit optimistic in their appraisals, a rapid jump would make them look fairly conservative a month or so down the line. Not long ago, yearly jumps of 30 to 40 percent were not uncommon in the Northeast. That is certainly no longer the case. And since the trend is downward in most regions, you can expect today's appraisers to be doubly cautious.

Think like an appraiser. You may be aware of properties similar to the one you're looking at that sold for a relatively high price a year or so ago, but you can't let that be your influencing factor. You must determine what that kind of home is selling for *today*. Again, don't be guided by asking prices; asking prices are just that. If a certain price is getting no buyers, all you can know for certain is that the market is below that figure.

You need to know the market fairly well; the appraiser will. His appraisal will be based on what has been sold recently, and that's all. It is entirely possible that you may suffer a big disappointment and learn that you're not going to get the mortgage you thought you would. In such a situation, you are faced with money problems once again.

If the additional money you needed was not for repayment of the purchase loan but for the additional funds required to make necessary improvements, you're not so badly off. You are a homeowner—you have a deed to prove it. You can do what your father and grandfather did and get a home improvement loan. The only potential snag is that this type of loan won't have a thirty-year term, so that loan payment in addition to a mortgage payment could be a bit difficult to manage.

If you're planning to make home improvements and intend to use a reputable, established contractor, you may find that the contractor can help you with the financing. There are longer-term FHA home improvement loans that are worth exploring.

You can ask about the FHA's ten-year home improvement loan program through regular banking sources. The program requires submission of plans and estimates to the FHA, but if you're working with the right contractor these will not be difficult to assemble. The ten-year term makes the loan affordable; a permanent loan plus this type of home improvement loan could overcome your financing problems.

Good financing: Key to successful real estate investment

Make it a point to become acquainted with the various types of mortgages available to you. Your decision can be influenced by your future plans. If you're looking to buy a home, raise a family, watch them grow up and move out, and stay in the home until you die, you'll be on the lookout for a certain kind of loan. (By the way, the majority of homeowners claim to feel that way, yet the statistics show that most keep their homes for seven years and then move.)

One new form of fixed-rate mortgage provides for a lower fixed rate for seven years. At the end of the seven-year term, it is adjusted to the prevailing market conditions. If you're planning to stay in the home for five years and then move on, that's probably the easiest way to go.

For some, a fixed-rate, thirty-year loan might be the best option; for others, an adjustable mortgage that starts out at a lower rate might be ideal. Bear in mind as you make your decision that adjustables can go down if rates go down. We've grown so accustomed to mortgage rates rising that the idea of adjustable rates dropping seems unreal, but drop they can. Adjustable rates depend on indices based on moneyed instruments, usually the index plus a set percentage above. When the moneyed instruments (treasury notes, for instance) take a downturn, so do the adjustable mortgages.

There are so many kinds of mortgage loans today that space prohibits me from offering detailed descriptions of them all. Many are FNMA or FHLMC programs, but there are banks that don't sell their adjustable mortgages in the secondary market. Their programs can be completely different from others being offered.

Shop around. Listen to what the lenders have to say. Analyze the various programs. And remember that if something sounds too good to be true, it probably is. There have been and probably still are loans offering lower rates and longer terms than most. The catch is that these loans peg the payments at a fixed amount, but the rate is variable. If the rate goes up, the unpaid interest is added to the principal balance. What does that mean? Well, if rates go up and you do not exercise your option to pay the sum separately, your mortgage balance goes up—and you can end up owing more than you started with!

The fancy name for that process is "negative amortization." There was a time some years back when this sort of arrangement was ideal for a potential homeowner who could not qualify for a higher rate. In an advancing market, it was not that big a risk. At any rate, the bank would usually alert you to the situation and inform you of your options. Today, the combination of negative amortization and declining home values could be catastrophic. I do not recommend that you obtain such a loan now.

The real estate market over the country follows the trends of the time.

There are always areas that will be more depressed than the mainstream of America due to economic circumstances.

The general trend since the end of World War Two has been a steady increase in home prices. You could generally expect an increase each year in your home value of 6 or 7 percent. There have been periods when there were tremendous jumps in home prices in certain vibrant areas. The closing years of the 1990s witnessed houses selling in prices that were higher than the original offering due to the high buyer demand.

When these rises occurred, they were followed by price declines. This factor made it difficult to sell the properties purchased during the increase period, because the mortgage often exceeded the value of the home. In a negative amortization mortgage, the accrued interest is added to the original principal amount, creating a debt that exceeds the original purchase price, because the mortgage often exceeded the value of the home. In a negative amortization mortgage, the accrued interest is added to the original principal amount, creating a debt that exceeds the original purchase price. You end up owing more than when you created the mortgage debt. If there is no inflationary trend to bring up the home value, you are in deep trouble. Stay away from these loans.

CHAPTER TEN

The Savings and Loan Debacle

The final debacle of the most recent millennium experienced revelations of bank officials granting loans to favored individuals that were far in excess of the property value.

The public was shocked by the extent of the venality of certain politicians and industry officials. The years of mismanagement and illicit activities in the savings and loan field have far-reaching repercussions; bailout costs will be staggering, running into the billions of dollars over a period of decades. The shady practices have had their greatest impact on the commercial real estate industry, but residential housing is also prominently featured in the portfolios of the offending institutions.

Often, unsound loans were granted to favored friends; when the downturn in the economy caused scores of buildings, malls, hotels, and other commercial structures to go bust, the lending institutions were left with large amounts of ORE that they were ill equipped to handle. Institutions failed. The Federal Savings and Loan Insurance Corporation was called in to make good on depositor funds. A trustee organization, called the Resolution Trust Corporation (RTC), now part of the FDIC, was created by the federal government to dispose of the properties to mitigate the loss to the government. The purpose of this body is to convert the foreclosed properties into liquid assets. The agency has offered its cooperation to responsible real estate brokers who will submit their qualifications and then be placed on the roster of cooperating sales brokers. Your broker may be one of the recognized agents.

Are you interested in real estate as a business? There may be properties in the RTC inventory that could be an attractive investment for you, although some of them may be a bit more complicated than you've dealt with. Start at a point where you feel comfortable with the tasks and responsibilities involved. If you already own numerous real estate investments, you may be ready to step up to one of these more sophisticated operations.

Consider the case of Harry Helmsley. His real estate portfolio was amassed during World War II. The nation was occupied with the winning of a war; wartime rent control measures were in full force. Real estate operators found themselves in a tough situation: They couldn't continue to operate under the ceilings set by the authorities. Many went under, and Helmsley found himself quite a few bargains. He never went in over his head, however. He proceeded judiciously and kept a close eye on his own cash position at all times. The same cannot be said for many of today's speculators.

Some prominent investors who were once hailed as financial wonders are in very deep trouble today. Most of them used a principle that works extremely well in real estate acquisitions when times are good: the practice of controlling a very large enterprise with a very small investment.

The term "leverage" comes from your high school physics class. Your teacher probably explained how difficult it is to dislodge a boulder with a two-by-four alone, but how easy it is once you place a wedge beneath the boulder. You make the two-by-four a lever, not just a board.

This is a fundamental law of physics—and a metaphor for a highly desirable rule of investing when the economy is growing. No doubt you've read or heard a great deal about leveraged buyouts. In these transactions, you use very little of your own money and take advantage of the availability of other people's money. Typically, you make some favorable arrangement with your seller that allows you to use his money as a loan, with the property as security.

In an expanding market, this is all well and good. But remember how we learned that money is a commodity, and that all commodities have a price? There is a price for the money used in a leveraged purchase, too.

Recall the hucksters on television eager to sell you on the idea of "no-money-down" real estate. One of the leading exponents of the practice wrote a bestselling book about it. He recently filed for bankruptcy. This even though he made a great deal from lecture fees and sales of his book! Imagine the size of the debt he must have amassed.

You *can* find reasonably safe ways to buy property for no money down, if you're familiar with certain techniques. Some sellers, such as a mortgagee or owner who is ready to walk away from a problem property, may well be willing to work with you without seeing a deposit.

These sellers would probably leap at the chance to sell, if only to get the town authorities or the board of health off their backs. Once you accept the deed, they're off the hook. Any payments you make to them under the agreement are gravy. If you default, they probably wouldn't even bother commencing a foreclosure action. (Ask yourself, though: How many of the properties the hucksters brag about on television fall into this category?)

The major problem with leveraged acquisitions is that they create 100 percent indebtedness. Although you have 100 percent ownership, you also have a debt ratio of 100 percent, which leaves you an equity of zero. Okay, you started with nothing. You do have the opportunity to turn the investment around and make a profit. That's good. But the downside is that if it's a neglected property you will have to cope with town authorities and neighbors. Remember, we're betting that the reason the seller gave you such generous terms is that he simply couldn't take it anymore. You may want to think twice about walking into such a situation.

Important: If there is no possibility of raising the return so that you have a positive cash flow, don't consider the property. No matter how tempting it may appear, you'll eventually regret buying. Experience has borne this principle out many times, so save yourself some heartache. If you're looking at a property you intend to hold and rent, and the income does not equal the outgo, *don't buy.*

The greatest activity in leveraged investments usually takes place when the economic community is humming and it looks like the expansion will never end. The market jumps, and suddenly you're the smartest kid on the block. You "flip," turning over the property for a profit. Congratulations! But . . .

The best laid plans can go awry. Leveraged purchases of hotels, department stores, airlines, and gaming establishments have been torpedoed by economic downturns. The same thing can happen to you. All the numbers, all the estimates, all the optimism will count for nothing. The profits never happened. The owners are stuck with enormous debt service. The piper wants payment—now.

One of the most successful, least flamboyant, least publicized real estate investors is San Francisco's largest commercial landlord, Walter Shorenstein. His advice, reported in *Forbes* magazine, is as follows: "Put at least 20% down. Have 10% in reserve to withstand pressures. You can't spend your last buck to buy a property." Good advice for prudent investors. I'd like to add a little of my own.

You can rest assured that every successful businessperson was once faced with the same kinds of choices you face. You can't play your cards too close to the vest; no one ever made a fortune saying "no" 100 percent of the time. (You can *save a fortune* this way, but you can't earn one.)

Make your decisions carefully. Sure, failure could really set you back. To paraphrase the song, though, you can always pick your business up, dust it off, and start all over again. It's not brain surgery. It's money.

The S&L offerings we're examining in this chapter could provide you with the opportunity to prosper from someone else's dusting-off-and-starting-over. I'm highlighting them here because of the basis on which the properties in question are being sold. It's not, "If we get X, we'll sell this property." It's, "How much can we get for this property?"

The people administering the properties are not real estate operators. They're temporary administrators whose job it is to maintain the properties as best they can until they can be transferred to permanent owners. Take a look at some of the offerings. If your credit is good, you may be able to spark some very good deals.

Someone who is "creditworthy" is, by definition, "worthy of being believed." If you have honored all your obligations as agreed—in other words, if you pay on time—you have good credit. We're dealing with real property, the loans for which are secured by mortgages. A mortgage payment record that shows prompt payment qualifies you for favored consideration.

If you have been a late payer on your mortgage and are contemplating making real estate investments that will require mortgage borrowing, change your habits for at least one year. That's the amount of time on record as a prompt payer the bank will want to see; some banks will ask to see copies of the checks.

Following up

You will become a winner in this field in much the same way as in any other: persistence. And that applies especially to your dealings with the Resolution Trust Corporation.

Once you call a broker who is registered with the RTC, he will politely take your name and tell you that he'll call you back when he has word of any interesting properties. Then he will never call. (Trust me; I speak from experience.)

It will be up to you to keep tabs on the properties coming up; call the local 800 number for the RTC listed in your phone book. Before too long, you'll come up with something and be advised (again) that you must work through a broker. You can then call your listless representative—who will spring back to life with remarkable speed. Should the sale ever come to fruition, the broker will brag to his co-workers about how he brought about the sale.

As it stands now, however, you are the one who wants to make the purchase. It's up to you to keep on top of things. The vast majority of real estate representatives cannot be counted on to aggressively look out for your interests and objectives.

I've been criticized about making remarks like that—not because people claim they're inaccurate (they're not) but because of the danger of polarizing the real estate community. Fortunately, every real estate broker believes himself to be one of the 5 percent who can be relied on to follow up, so the danger of polarization is really minimal.

Take my advice and carry the ball yourself. You keep in touch. Even if you're told by your representative that your offer is unacceptable, try to find out *directly* if there's some compromise that will make everyone happy.

Why am I telling you to bypass your agent? Because I know for a fact that far too many of them have never learned to counter objections or elicit counteroffers. You're dealing with a government agency that *must* get rid of a huge number of problem properties. If what you propose is unacceptable, what would the RTC entertain? How can it be resolved? Sometimes you may have to ask to speak to someone higher up. Do so. Don't give up.

I've seen these cast-aside situations turned into successful transfers because one of the parties didn't initially understand the full significance of the other person's position. When you get to speak to the other party, you may learn that his perception of what you offered was completely different from what you had intended. Only by speaking with him will you have the opportunity to correct such misperceptions.

Avoiding emotion in purchasing investment property

If you're getting turned down, competition may well be a factor. A cautionary note is in order here: If you're obliged to change your offer because someone wants to pay more, don't rush into the fray to compete. You're dealing with investment property. If it's not a good deal for you at the upper figure, let the competitor buy it.

Never fall in love with an investment because of its prestige or appearance, or for any other reason. So the building is beautiful, so what? Some of the most profitable real estate investments feature unattractive facilities that cause many to bypass them as opportunities. And some gorgeous properties are "alligators": They'll eat you alive. Many of the RTC's offerings will present a very desirable appearance. Still, you must ask yourself: "What will it yield me?" "Can I turn it over at a higher price?"

Emotional appeals have no place in investment property. These deals must be analyzed solely by means of cold, hard logic. I think some of the headline-grabbing acquisitions of the past couple of years are now showing the validity of this principle. Don't get hypnotized; don't let someone flatter you into making a bad investment.

Find out how much operating income the property will generate. "Net operating income" means gross income less operating expenses, less debt service, taxes, and so on. What is referred to as the bottom line is actually net operating income, or N.O.I.

Get expert advice when you can, and especially if you are entering a field of endeavor with which you are unfamiliar. (But remember that a bank teller is not the best "expert" on banking practices, and the mere fact that someone possesses a real estate license proves nothing about that person's skill in dealing with investment properties.) Get the best counsel you can, then make your decision.

CHAPTER ELEVEN

Investment Real Estate

There are many dos and don'ts when it comes to investment real estate. I'd like to pass a few along to you.

Research

Before you decide to buy a foreclosed property, do the research. Ask questions of people who would provide the services that you need. By that I mean you should speak to an oil company, a plumber, and/or a general contractor. After all, if you were to go on a trip, you'd probably get a bunch of maps. You'd then chart your course and figure out how long it would take you to reach each stop. You'd then want to calculate what food and lodging would be required at each stage. You'd provide for rest stops, food stops, tolls, and road conditions you might encounter. You wouldn't sit down in your car, turn the key, and say to yourself, "I'll go north for a bit and see where it takes me, then I'll ask for further directions." If you're buying what is basically a problem property, try to get the answers for the problems before you encounter them. You want to be able to react appropriately when the time comes.

When I was working with HUD, I used to take a checklist with me and inspect the property. I had experience with my rental management housing in ordering repairs as they were needed. I wasn't an expert, but I was able to come up with ballpark figures that would give a general idea of what was needed.

If you can gain entry to the property being foreclosed, you'll have an important advantage. If you can't get inside, an inspection of the exterior could give you an idea of what to expect. If the outside is bad, you can expect the interior to need work, as well.

You can tell a lot from looking at the outside of a house. You can spot rotting window frames, bad door jambs, and roof and gutter problems. You might even be able to spot termite damage or dry rot. Of course, the driveway and walks are also spots to check.

What costs the most to repair or replace? Plumbing, heating systems, electrical systems, termite repair, and roof repair. Still, you shouldn't necessarily let problems in these areas scare you away. Everything comes down to dollars: for materials, for labor, for holding time. If the dollars are all there and you still have a cushion, a safety amount in reserve, you're on the right track.

Pay a visit to the kitchen cabinet and bathroom replacement centers. Price a few typical systems that would be likely replacement purchases. Ask the salesperson how much installation would cost. If you don't get any good information, you may be able to pick up the cards of installers or plumbers.

If you have to, call the plumber. "Your card was passed along to me by Joe of Custom Kitchen Cabinets. I'm interested in that 19-foot Kensington model they have. Could you give me a general idea of how much something like that would cost to install?" (You can ask him about the heating systems, too.)

A good plumber can be real asset in your decision-making process, as can a qualified electrician. You might ask the electrician about the general figure for conversion to 150-amp service or a similar setup.

Roofers will quote dollars per "square" (a unit equal to three bundles of shingles). You'll be able to find out how many squares are typically required for the type of home you're purchasing. Floors, too, are often in need of repair. If you're dealing with tiles, go through the same routine. As for windows, you'll find that the most popular models can be bought and installed for a set sum that is fairly easy to isolate.

Contrary to what you might think, repair of broken walls and ceilings is usually no big deal; the same holds true for tiled bathrooms that need work. Some of the most horribly vandalized properties are restored for less than you'd imagine possible. This is the reason you should not be turned off instantly by broken windows, walls, pipes, and so on. A contractor knows what's needed—even if you don't—and can order the supplies, select the proper tools, do the work, and get in and out fast. When it's all done, you'll be looking at the work of a professional, and you probably won't have paid as much as you first feared you would.

Time

Throughout this period, you may well be paying a higher rate of interest on your hard money loan. Taxes and insurance have to be paid, too. You want to speed things up. Your acquisition cost actually includes the cost of money, taxes, insurance, and related expenses incurred during the renovation. The longer it takes you to complete the job, the more it's going to cost you. (There is also the all-too-common problem of vandalism during the periods the property is empty.)

Make your own checklist; I've included one in the appendix section of this book for you to use as a guide. Itemize as I've outlined and add whatever else you think is needed. If the house is occupied, figure that you may have to get a lawyer to evict, so estimate the cost of the delay and the court action. Add everything up. If you had to spend all that you had to bring the house into livable condition, would it be worth the bid price you thought you'd go to? Will it be valued at that figure by the appraiser? Would you be able to get the mortgage you need?

Let's assume now that, armed with this information, you went to the sale and acted accordingly. Now it's your property, and your objective is to get it into usable condition as soon as humanly possible. Of course, if you're going to move into it, you're going to put a great deal of thought into customizing your home—but if you're not going to move into it, you should be particularly careful to avoid making the mistake of doing a halfway job.

You may feel that a tenanted property is not at all like a home you yourself would want to live in, that it need only be "good enough" to attract the lower element of the rental market. There's a problem with this reasoning: The lower you go, the higher your risk as a landlord. If you put together a unit that will only attract renters who will take anything, whose sole goal is to get a roof over their heads, you'll pay for it in the end. It is entirely possible that your new occupants will have a poor history as tenants. Even "references" from relatives or present landlords are suspect. Relatives will cover for their own; landlords want to get rid of people who don't pay their bills. Don't inherit someone else's problem. Bring the unit up to par. Your goal should be to attract a tenant who *wants* to move in, not someone who has no other choice.

Problem tenants

I imagine I've heard just about every song-and-dance from bad rental risks that there is. Here's an assortment of problem cases I've learned to avoid from bitter experience.

Tellers of tales of woe. Inexplicable bad luck seems to stalk them wherever they go. They are very good at eliciting sympathy, very good at proving the legitimacy of the latest disaster. They're not so good at coming up with rent payments. They expect you to understand the seriousness of this week's dilemma and patiently hold off your request for rent "until this blows over." That's always at some indeterminate point in the future.

Proclaimed fixer-uppers. As they're applying, they'll say something like, "I'm very handy; how would you feel about me making a room out of that unfinished attic up there?" You'll think it's your lucky day: a tenant is actually going to help you increase the value of your property. But it's all baloney. He knows what you want to hear and he's letting you hear it in the hope you'll ignore or overlook a bad credit record or previous problems with landlords. Scratch the surface and you'll almost certainly find a deadbeat. Ask him if he'll permit you to order a credit check and/or get his social security number.

If you do this, one of two things can happen. He may tell you that he left all his personal papers with his sister/partner/whoever is in Florida/Canada/wherever and that he's going to have them mailed to him once he has an address. Or he may decide he can't con you and tell you that although he likes your place better, he'll have to take the other place he's looking at since that landlord is prepared to take him as is. There is no other place; he's trying to prey on your desire to have the unit occupied. Call his bluff. Wish him good luck and show him the door.

Welfare tenants. I know it may sound elitist or high-handed, but the fact is these situations just carry too much risk to work out happily for you. A broker may well try to talk you into accepting these tenants because the welfare agency will pay the rent to you like clockwork every month. So what? The problem is that the majority of people on welfare have no regard for your property rights. I'm not talking here about people who are momentarily down on their luck and who accept welfare only as a last resort. I'm talking about the majority, the second-, third-, or even fourth-generation welfare families who have never known any other existence. Too many people in this category have no regard for order, for cleanliness, or for property rights. They are, in short, very bad risks.

Everything breaks. Everything goes wrong. You spend vast amounts of time solving problems you never expected, repairing stoves, fixing things that shouldn't have broken in the first place. A former partner of mine once astutely observed that welfare tenants, on the whole, "consume buildings." Nobody likes that, but it is so.

I had a welfare tenant in one of the houses on Donegan Avenue. I managed; I hardly ever saw the house because the welfare agency sent me the rent. One day I got a call from the Department of Health ordering me to fix the plumbing at the house. I had received no word from the tenant that there was anything wrong with the plumbing or anything else. I went over with my plumber to check the problem out.

Out in the yard was a mountain of plastic garbage bags that had somehow never made it to the curb for pickup. I don't want to guess how long the collection had been building. Once we made it into the kitchen, we saw still more bags of garbage lying in heaps all around the kitchen. Cockroaches were everywhere.

We entered the bathroom and found that the commode had been broken, as had the wash basin. I made arrangements for these to be replaced and left the house.

Two weeks later another call came from the Department of Health instructing me to fix the plumbing at the same address. I assured them that there was some problem with the records, since I had just had the plumbing fixed at that site. The caller insisted that I had to repair the plumbing, however, and so I went to the house for the second time. Sure enough, the brand new commode had been broken less than a month after having been installed.

Here's another example. My partner and I fixed up a twenty-eight-unit complex, supplying new kitchens, windows, aluminum storm doors, and so on. Each unit was separated by chain link fences to protect the new landscaping we'd done. When we'd finished, we looked with some satisfaction at a charming little enclave, ready for occupants, where once a set of devastated buildings had been.

The tenancy was 90 percent welfare. We watched in disbelief as, day by day, the property disintegrated before our eyes. Within one month, the fences were torn away from the posts, the storm doors were off the hinges, the plants were ripped out, and graffiti adorned our newly painted walls. No one in the building was in any way concerned about the destruction. My partner and I were outraged.

Welfare is the county's problem. Don't ask for a share. I say that with the understanding that the problems of which I'm speaking encompass all races, nationalities, and creeds. People on welfare, as a group, tend to cause conditions that compel owners to walk away from properties. That's not to say that I haven't had good tenants who were on welfare; I have. But they were very much in the minority. Our goal here is to identify potential problem tenants, and this group is a prime supplier of them.

To be sure, there are a good many low-life slumlords out there who aren't helping matters. But there are also many well-meaning individuals who start out with the belief that if you give people a nice place to live they'll maintain it, even if they're not well off. Those well-meaning individuals usually get hurt financially. My partner and I were lucky; we got out in time. But many well-intentioned people lose huge amounts of money and even receive bad publicity when characterized as slumlords by reporters out to file an exciting story. I hope you don't have to go through any of that.

There are much better avenues of investment open to you. Remember, real estate investment carries with it the burden of real estate management. Your goal should be to make sure the burden is a manageable one.

CHAPTER TWELVE

Managing Investment Real Estate

The appeal of owning real property and having tenants who are paying off your indebtedness (mortgage loan) for you appeals to most people looking to accumulate wealth. It is probably true that more wealth has been acquired through real estate holdings than using other mediums.

There is just one problem. In my fifty years of real estate experience, I have discovered that a vast number of tenants just do not pay on time. Not only do they not pay on time, but they create other costly problems for the property owner that far outweigh the benefits.

I have never seen figures so I cannot tell you that the majority of renters are poor payers, but the number who do not pay on time are so vast that they merit an examination.

Many renters are renting only because they are not sure that they are going to remain in the area or they would like to become acquainted with the area first and then decide where they will reside. These are the tenants you should welcome. They are homeowners at heart and will usually treat a rental unit in the same manner as they would their home.

On the other hand, the woods are full of people who do not have the wherewithal to purchase a home. They have never been able to put aside money for anything. Owning a home is something they never expect to achieve. The first big problem is that the rent payment is the largest of their obligations. They cannot pay it in extended payments and so it is the last thing they pay each month. Meeting a due date is difficult. So they are late. In the meantime you have been counting on the payment in order to make your mortgage payment. When you do not receive it on schedule, it creates a difficult situation for you. You cannot tell this to your tenant because, "since you are a landlord, you must be rich." Because you are rich, you are expected to empathize with the tenant. You will now discover that your tenant has had a particular stretch of bad luck. Not only that, he will tell you that his brother-in-law was in a terrible accident and he had to loan him his saved dollars. It is amazing how charitable and kindly these people are. They are always helping some member of their family. Of course, because you are rich you should be able to give him a little extra time.

The real estate industry opened my eyes to so many things. As I discuss what will follow, I may appear hardhearted and unmindful of the misery in this world. Well, what I am sharing with you today are the experiences I have had personally with real estate investments. They are not theory. They are actual.

I attended a highly liberal college. In those days, I felt very deeply about the tragedies of the poor, downtrodden masses. When I crossed over to the other side of the interview, I discovered that there are people who are winners and there are people who are losers. The caution is that when you become a landlord, you must learn to recognize these losers. You would be better off with a three-month vacancy than accepting these people. They will destroy you. I wrote previously about my experiences with the house on Donegan Avenue which was only one of many I had like it.

In the first place, let me caution you:

- Do not become involved with welfare tenants. They have never owned property and damaging property is quite acceptable to them.
- Do not accept tenants under the Section 8 Rental Assistance program. This program subsidizes low-income family rentals. The problem is that the agency doesn't always permit the price that you are asking. You may get a tenant who is willing to pay the overage to you "under the table." If you go along with this you are committing a fraud against the U.S. government. Don't ever involve yourself in such a situation. If the agency won't change its ruling, find another tenant.

Every now and then your TV will show tenants living in apartment houses with holes in the wall, garbage in the hallways, and numerous other horrible conditions. Who broke the walls? Who threw the garbage in the hallway plus all the other indecencies? The tenants! If you dig deeper, you may find that the owner is a plumber who saved up and had an opportunity to get what he thought was a great deal on an apartment house. He tried. He fixed. He exhausted his savings and now in disgust he is letting it go to foreclosure. In the meantime the TV exposé is calling him a slumlord. Do you need that? Do not get started with that type of tenancy. You cannot win. You are going to get deeper into debt.

The same advice goes for purchasing a two-family house with the idea of getting the income for the rental to pay toward your mortgage. If you want a two-family to house two units of your family, that is one thing. If you are looking for the income, look at it this way: You are paying a higher price for a two-family house. In addition, the taxes are higher, so your mortgage payment is more. Now if the tenant does not pay or is slow in payment, you are living with him. It is an unpleasant circumstance.

I have always counseled, "If you are going to be a landlord, be a big one. It is like buying a mutual fund rather than a single stock. You have a cushion against losses. Two-family house in which you are to occupy one unit? No! No! No!

Let us get on to some tips on how you can protect yourself and get your rent on time.

You may or may not sign a lease with your tenant. The best course is to sign a lease. It spells everything out. If you are compelled to go to court for any reason whatsoever, it is best to have it spelled out. If you are seeking to enforce it, the court must hold with you because you have a contract (lease) and there is no other consideration. Stationery stores sell prepared lease forms. There are simple computer software programs also available. All you need to do is fill in the blanks.

In recent years, some landlords have written late charges into the agreement if the rent payment is not received on time. Some courts may question your right to levy this. My recommendation is this. Let us say that you want to get a rental amount of $675. Offer the unit at $715. Now, if you are going to advertise it, you can advertise it at $675 and tell the renter, "I must explain that the rental is $715 and my lease will state that amount. I will, however, have the following clause in the lease: Provided that the rental payment is received by 5:00 P.M. on the fifth day of each month the tenant will be granted a discount of $40 with such payment."

The difference is that you have an agreement for $715. If you have to take him to court, you are seeking $715, not $675. You are not charging a late charge. You are offering a discount, and it will stand up in court because that is the contracted figure. If the prospect balks at this arrangement, thank him for answering your ad and show him the door.

Today with credit checks and social security numbers, you can get an immediate report on a prospect's record. A word of caution is needed here. If there is no record available on a person well past his early years, he could very well have given a false number. If he claims to have never had credit experience, turn him down. Do not get involved.

Checking references is another caution. If the reference is a personal one, he could have given you his friend's number. What about his previous landlord? He may be anxious to get rid of him so he will not give you any adverse reports.

You have to be the psychologist. As I told you earlier, if he is offering to improve your property in some way, your antenna should go up. It should make you want to check him much more closely. He is giving you the romance. I know. I was taken in with it the first time that I encountered such a generous soul. If it is possible for you to arrange a meeting with him at his present domicile, this would be best. You would be able to get an idea of how he is going to treat your property.

If you come across anything in the credit check that is adverse, do not think that you can compensate by taking an additional security deposit. When you have bad experience with a tenant, you will find that the wheels of justice grind slowly and your time buffer disintegrates.

Should your lease commence after the first day of the month, calculate the amount for the partial month and have the full amount due on the first of every month thereafter. It is much better for your bookkeeping.

The person who tells you that he just moved into town may be telling you the truth. Look at his license plates. Are they from out of state, as he claims? The experienced con artists I have met claimed that they took a job out of state, but then decided against it.

There are so many ways that you can check up. Explore them all before you turn over a key to your property. Make sure that he is who he says he is. Check his license and any other identification. Once you have surrendered the premises to an individual, you are in your weakest position. You can only remove him through due process of law and that can be time consuming.

I have warned you about welfare tenants and others of the same general economic circumstances. After you have warned them and have resorted to the legal process, you are going to meet another character you would do well to avoid. Since they are underprivileged, they have the privilege of contacting the Legal Aid Society. This representative believes that all landlords are evil and are enriching themselves at the expense of these poor underprivileged souls who want nothing more then to live in nice warm places where they can enjoy peace and harmony. You are now served with an "order to show cause." This is nothing more than a stalling device employed by the legal beagles to give their clients time to find some other poor soul who will turn over his well-kept domicile to these disruptive clients. You will now discover that (according to the complaint) there is no water, no fuel (if you provide it), a broken stove, etc. This is your first notice of anything being wrong with the premises. They always occur after you start your action. Fortunately, the judges are aware of this device and eventually you will get them out. But this has cost in lost rent and additional legal expenses.

Have I made my point clear? You cannot change these people. Not only do they not respect property, they see landlords as the enemy who is out to suck their blood.

Exaggeration? They have voiced these sentiments to me many times. Invest in real estate, but make sure that you have investigated the prospective tenants' records. Get a good tenant and you will enjoy the fruits of your investment.

Good luck!

CHAPTER THIRTEEN

Calculating a Bid Price for Investment Property

In determining what you want to bid for a property, you must take into consideration the use to which it will be put. Someone intending to live in the property can be expected to pay more than someone seeking to use it for investment purposes. It is the investment-type bid we will be examining here.

You intend to turn the property over for a profit, and quickly. I recommend that you consider using real estate brokers to help you sell; you can use all the exposure you can get. Brokers with multiple listing services can provide the broader coverage.

Allow time in your calculations. Even under the most favorable conditions, time has a habit of slipping away. Unforeseen delays are costly, yet they do occur and you must provide for them.

If you're going to do work or have work done for you, make sure that you establish deadlines. Make it absolutely clear that payment depends on adhering to those completion dates. Contractors have a habit of starting several jobs at once and delaying all of them while they seek new business.

Never make the mistake of giving a large advance deposit to a contractor. If he runs a small business and tells you that he needs funds to buy materials, have him select the materials and have them shipped to you. Then you pay the supplier. At least you have the materials if commencement of the project drags on indefinitely.

Remember: While the property is unoccupied, you are paying for the cost of money, for taxes, and for insurance. Figure these elements into your calculations. I usually use six months as a time frame and would not advise cutting it any shorter unless the property needs no work whatsoever. If there's a lot to be done, you might do well to extend the time frame to nine months.

Start at the top. How much do you think the property would be worth if you brought it to tip-top condition? Can you price it slightly below the market so it moves more quickly than other comparable homes for sale?

Isolating the repairs that will add the most value

For a property that you're intending to resell, I'd suggest you pay particularly close attention to the kitchen and bathroom. These are the areas of the house that draw the greatest interest. Beyond that, if you can carpet the floors, do so. Get a neutral color carpet that will blend with many decors.

I don't advise that you panel the walls. There was a time when paneling was all the rage, but today it has fallen into disfavor. You're better off simply painting the walls in a neutral gray or beige.

With a property that needs sprucing up, don't make the mistake of putting off painting because "people will want to choose their own colors." Your objective is to avoid negative perceptions and comments from potential buyers. Believe me, you'll get back every dollar of your expenditure in higher selling price and reduced waiting time.

Other cost concerns

With respect to the costs of sale through your real estate agent, each locality has its own standards. Commissions are set by agreement. You should speak to a local realtor and determine an average rate from him.

Legal charges are also established by agreement. Your lawyer could advise you as to his fee for handling the transaction. (A good realtor can also be depended on to recommend a lawyer known to charge reasonable fees.)

Stamps on deeds are either state- or local-revenue charges. Practices differ from area to area. Charges for preparing and recording a mortgage satisfaction piece, as well as a title closer gratuity, can also be determined from your attorney or realtor. There may be other charges these professionals can point out to you.

Title insurance charges and costs for recording the deed from the foreclosure purchase can be secured from a title company.

Holding costs is an area in which many prospective investors get hurt. Be sure you provide for taxes, insurance, the cost of money, and utilities during the holding period.

Take the checklists at the end of this book with you when you examine the property. See if you can estimate what is needed; allow yourself a reasonable figure to accomplish whatever must be done. Estimate high.

Even if you're going to do some of the work yourself, estimate what a professional would charge and use that figure. You might plan initially to take care of certain items only to find that you don't have the time, inclination, or skill. Give yourself a cushion; budget as though you're planning on using a professional. Talk to the plumbers, painters, installers, or whoever and get a ballpark estimate to work with. (Note that a painter will give you a per room cost and an exterior cost.)

Armed with all this information, you'll be able to set the upper limit of your bid. The final checklist in the back of this book, "Overall Cost of Purchase," should tell you all you need to know. (Of course, if you find that there is no profit, you should not make the bid at all!)

Making the choices

All of the foregoing applies to speculative purchases only. As we learned a little earlier, a different set of standards will apply to a home you intend to occupy yourself. Of course, you can still use the checklists at the back of this book to give you an idea whether you should buy a foreclosed property to fix up or buy a house in good condition with all the amenities.

CHAPTER FOURTEEN

Those No-Cash Infomercials

Our TV screens bombard us with offers to teach us how to get rich in real estate with no cash outlay. I referred in a prior chapter to one of those authors who wrote about the process. I also told you that I read that he had filed for bankruptcy.

Well, let us analyze all these offers. After all, they show you interviews with people of less means than you who tell you of the fantastic deals they have made.

Let us start with the no-cash aspect first. I will grant you that you can get such deals, but let us deal with the very first part.

In return for your no-cash acquisition, you are giving the vendor something. He is not transferring his property to you for no consideration of any kind. I will again grant you that it may be possible to obtain that type of deal, too. We will look at that as well. You will probably sign a bond or note of some sort, or you may be giving back a second mortgage. I am assuming that there was an existing mortgage on the property, because I cannot imagine any seller of property taking back a mortgage for the entire debt. But, then again, it may be possible too, and when we address these later, we will have a better idea of why it was done this way.

So, let us begin with the process. You have put no cash down. So you now have a 100 percent debt position. If you have acquired the property to live in yourself, that is one scenario. If you have acquired it for investment, that is a different one. If the seller had a high existing mortgage, chances are that the payments to the bank are high to begin with. Now, if he is taking back a second mortgage for that part of his price that is more than the mortgage amount, that will require repayment.

Let's take an example:

You have seen a house that has an existing 7 1/2 percent mortgage on it. The payments are $1,080. That is based on a principal and interest payment of $697 on the principal amount of $83,000 originally and now reduced to $80,000. Taxes differ in all areas, but let us assume $4,000 a year or $333 per month plus $50 per month for a homeowners policy. He wants to recover his original $3,000 and will take back a second mortgage at the same 7 1/2 percent rate. That adds $33.39, bringing your payment up to $1,113.39 per month for fifteen years and $1,080 per month for the remainder of the term.

If you are going to live in the house, this could be acceptable to you because you are purchasing a home with no money down and you are paying out your down payment over a period of fifteen years. The chances are that if you were looking to rent a similar house in the area, you might find one for $950 to

$1,000 per month, but this way you are buying, not renting, and you get tax benefits.

Now let us consider buying it for investment. You have got to find a tenant for something in excess of $1,113 per month. Even if you were lucky enough to find one, just remember, one month's vacancy could devastate you. So, face it. This type of no-cash deal is fraught with alligators.

But before I get into any other examples, let us cover a very important point right now. Before World War II, America was a country of renters. With the GI Bill and the Federal Housing Administration, the real estate market was opened wide. Houses could be bought for no cash down by a veteran and 3 percent down by a nonveteran. House hunting became a national pastime. The greatest advantage of those mortgages was that they could be transferred to a new buyer with no credit check to the buyer. As time went on and houses were sold subject to the existing mortgage, the banks found themselves boxed in with low interest rate mortgages. New mortgages were being offered at higher rates, and so many buyers at that time, even those with good credit, sought out homes being offered with existing GI or FHA mortgages.

To counter the continuance of the process, the banks now instituted a new change in their mortgage loan offerings. It was called "due on sale." This meant that if you sold your house with a mortgage, you would have to contact your bank. The bank did not really want it to be due on sale. It wanted to adjust the mortgage to the existing mortgage conditions. It also wanted a credit statement from the new purchaser. If mortgage rates had increased and the purchaser's credit was good, the bank would permit him to assume the existing mortgage and would now transfer the mortgage debt to the new purchaser but at the current rate.

If rates at the time of the sale had fallen, the bank would permit the mortgage debt to be transferred at the original rate. Rightly so. If the original mortgagor was not selling, the bank would not have reduced his rate. Now the importance of all the foregoing is that if you are being offered an existing mortgage to assume, you have got to obtain the bank's approval. If you take it over and do not notify the bank, you can get a very unpleasant surprise. When the bank becomes aware of the transfer without its consent, it can call the mortgage "due on sale." Pay up. No excuses.

How do those infomercial teachers treat that? Do they tell you to just ignore it?

So now let us move on to another point. There are tens of thousands of practicing real estate brokers and salespersons. How come they are not scooping up all these bargains before you get a chance to do so?

Believe it or not, there are many real estate opportunities that are absolutely worthless. In a prior chapter, I told you a story about a property I owned where tenants broke everything almost as soon as I installed it. If I had known of these "no money down" deals, I could have found some sucker to take the alligator off my hands. If I arranged for my purchaser to make payments to me, any such payments I might have received would have been a gift. I had bought it subject to the existing mortgage and had no responsibility for it. So I walked away. It never affected my credit.

How many of these wonderful deals being offered for no cash down are similar to this type? There is a case of a New York bank that had a mortgage on an apartment building in

Manhattan. I do not know anything about the owners, but I am sure they had the same types of problems as I had with those bad tenants. They just had more of them. The owners walked away from the building. Now there was no heat, no electric, no maintenance, and the tenants contacted Legal Aid. Legal Aid went to work. The court ordered the bank to provide the services. Just think. The bank did not own the building. It was the number one creditor. Now, I ask you: Do you think you could make a terrific deal with the bank if you wanted to buy it?

The reason I tell you of these instances is because these are the type of deals you can expect for "no cash down." They are out there.

If you are a contractor, plumber, or electrician, you might feel that you could go in and change things. You are like the young woman who proposes to marry a man who is a cheat, a philanderer, and a manipulator. She believes she can change him. You stand just as much a chance of succeeding as she does. The fact is that if someone is willing to take a no cash down deal, it is because he is in a bind and must do so. Well, here again, I get back to a point I have been stressing. If you have good credit, it could be possible. You would have to be approved by the bank in order to take over the mortgage. Based on this, the seller could be convinced to give you a second mortgage with no cash down. But as an investment property, no go.

When you buy for no cash down, you have pledged yourself to repay a 100 percent debt. Although you own it, you have no equity. As long as you can make the payments, you have no problems.

What they tell you to do, if you are an investor, is to take a property that you own, create a second mortgage on it, and carry it with you. You offer it as a down payment on the property you intend to buy. Let's assume that it is a $10,000 second mortgage. It provides for payments to be made at an agreeable rate. Now you can get a mortgage from a lender, maybe even the seller himself. He is slightly more secure than a 100 percent mortgage. He has $10,000 he can invest in a different property plus he can take back the property he just sold you and have a bit of salvage through the other security. It is this type of thinking that gets you into trouble. You have 100 percent debt, and if there are any downturns in the economy or the rental market, the whole pyramid can tumble. I've seen it happen many times.

When things are good in the real estate market and market values are climbing steadily, you cannot make a mistake. When the economy is down, the 100 percent debt is stifling.

APPENDIX A

The Most Commonly Asked Questions

Following are answers to some of the most commonly posed questions regarding purchases of foreclosures and related issues.

Q. Are there closing costs when buying a foreclosure?

A. Yes: the cost of the title insurance policy and the cost of recording your deed.

Q. Will I need a lawyer when buying a foreclosure?

A. There's really not much a lawyer can do for you at the sale itself. The terms are set; the lawyer will not be able to change them. Your title insurance policy is the best protection.

Q. Once you put your bid in at the foreclosure sale, can the homeowner still get the property back before you put down the balance?

A. No. Once the sale goes forth, it is final.

Q. I'm concerned about the permanence of the foreclosure sale I'm contemplating. Doesn't the former owner have the right to buy the house back within a year?

A. That's what's known as a "right of redemption." Such rights do not exist in foreclosure sales, although they do in tax sales or sheriff's sales. See the earlier chapters on foreclosure sales and tax sales for more information on these transactions.

Q. How do you get people out of the property if they continue to occupy after the sale? Won't the bank take care of that?

A. The bank will not handle this for you. You'll have to go to court. This situation is similar to a tenant holdover conflict in which a landlord wishes to eject a tenant from a rental property. You'll need the marshal or sheriff, whichever your county uses, to remove them legally. This could be difficult in a rent-controlled area. Talk to your attorney.

Q. Can I get a GI mortgage on a foreclosure?

A. Not on a foreclosed property bought at public auction. You must pay in full within 30 days; you cannot buy the property with a financing contingency. Such sales are "all cash," although you might be able to get a GI mortgage on a bank-owned foreclosure. That is up to the bank.

Q. Why shouldn't banks look forward to selling out properties with small mortgages so they can make money on the sale?

A. ORE (Owned Real Estate) is an item banks would rather not have on their financial statements. They'd much prefer to have these properties sold to third parties. Banks can collect only the sums legally due them. They do not share in any overage that may arise from the property.

Q. I've gone to a house that was in the process of being foreclosed, but the occupant wouldn't let me in to see the place. How can I get a look before placing a bid?

A. If you were in the other person's shoes, you wouldn't want to let anyone in, either. You may be limited to an exterior assessment. On the other hand, if the house is vacant, you can always try calling the bank. You'll probably get in for a look; after all, the bank wants to sell the property.

Q. Where can I learn about properties being foreclosed?

A. If there is no publication in your area that covers these matters, you can go to the county courthouse where the notices are posted. Look through your newspapers as well. You will find public notices there.

Q. Where are foreclosure sales held?

A. The notice of publication will indicate where the sale will be held. Typically, sales are held on the steps of the courthouse. As noted earlier in this book, when the notice states that the sale will be held "on the courthouse steps," it really does mean the physical outdoor steps leading into the building. If you are confused about location, call ahead or ask security personnel for help. You must be prompt in arriving at foreclosure sales.

Q. Let's assume that I am the successful bidder at the sale. Am I obligated to pay up any other creditors of the party being foreclosed?

A. Only if the recording of their claims precedes the recording of the party who is doing the foreclosure.

Q. Suppose that a second mortgage is being foreclosed and that I win the bid. Do I have to pay up the first mortgage completely?

A. No, although if it is in arrears you will have to bring it current. You assume the responsibility for it when you buy the property at the foreclosure sale.

Q. If I win the bid and someone turns up with a legitimate claim on the property, do I have to pay it?

A. If you mean by "legitimate" that the claim precedes the foreclosing party's claim bid and was missed on the title search, the answer is no—as long as you have title insurance. The title insurance company is on the hook for such a claim. This scenario is exactly what you are paying to avoid when you buy title insurance.

Q. Will the bank put in a new stove? Reupholster the furniture? Fix the neglect of the past owner?

A. All of these "will the bank" questions—and many others—aren't likely to be answered the way you'd hope. The bank won't do anything to property it doesn't own except board it up to prevent vandalism. If you buy a previously foreclosed property from the bank's ORE, that's a different story. In such a case, the bank owns the property. You can ask for anything. The answer you get will depend on the individual circumstances surrounding the property.

Q. If a property is being foreclosed, could I arrange to buy it before the sale from the owner and continue his mortgage?

A. If you could get an agreement for a deed from the mortgagor, you could talk to the bank about reinstating the mortgage and assuming it. If you're a good credit risk, you can probably manage this.

Important: Make sure there is no other recorded debt against the property

Q. I'd like to simplify things. Is there a rule of thumb to help me determine what percentage of value I should pay for a foreclosure?

A.   No. Too many variables—condition, salability, location, financing, and taxes, to name only a few—come into play.

Q.   **My state has very favorable mortgage rates for a first-time buyer, and I'd like to take advantage of them. If I buy in at the sale, can I then apply for the first-time buyer's rate?**

A.   Unfortunately, the answer here is probably not an encouraging one for you. If you buy at the sale and then look for the mortgage, you're refinancing and will *not* be considered a first-time buyer.

Note: You may want to look into the possibility of having a relative make the purchase for you, then paying back the amount spent once you get your first-time mortgage. This may be easier than you think if your relative is willing to take out a home equity loan for the purpose of this relatively brief transaction.

Q.   **If the foreclosed property has improvements that were never finally inspected and there are no certificates of occupancy for them, will the bank furnish these certificates at the sale?**

A.   No. This is one of the perils of buying a foreclosure. In order to get a permanent mortgage loan on the property, you will have to get the certificates. This is usually not a major setback, but you will have to do some legwork and handle the minor expenses associated with the process.

Q. **I have a friend who's a plumber; he'll inspect, for free, the house I have my eye on. Can I bring him into any house I want to bid on?**

A. If the people in possession will let you in, yes. If they won't, no. The current occupants are under no obligation to permit you to inspect.

Q. **What are the rights of tenants under a lease?**

A. If the lease precedes the date of the mortgage being foreclosed, the tenant stays. Leases made after this date are invalidated by the foreclosure process. Consult your attorney for more details; remember that local laws (and approaches) will vary when it comes to extricating tenants from property to which you have a legal right.

Q. **I've heard that the real estate brokers have an inside track on the good foreclosures. Is this true?**

A. The only edge they have is their knowledge of the market. They will probably recognize a good buy before someone unfamiliar with the real estate environment in which they work.

Q. **I've heard that novice buyers sometimes face a stacked deck when attempting to buy foreclosed properties from the bank. Is this true? Do banks show favoritism toward certain bidders at an auction sale?**

A. Foreclosure sales are conducted by a referee who is assigned by the court. The bank has no say in the selection of this person.

Q. **If the prior owner didn't pay the taxes on a foreclosed property, does the successful bidder have to pay them?**

A. No. If the taxes weren't paid, the county could sell the property out from under the bank's mortgage lien. Banks pay the amounts due to municipalities and sell the property with all tax payments current.

Q. **How does a tax sale differ from a foreclosure sale?**

A. When the public authorities offer a property for sale to satisfy a tax lien, the successful bidder buys the right to own the property *if the property owner does not repay him*. This is not the case at a foreclosure sale.

APPENDIX B

Checklists

Exterior

	Estimated Cost
Driveway, Walks	$_____
Shrubbery, Lawn	$_____
Rubbish Removal	$_____
Screens and Storm Windows	$_____
Chimney	$_____
Window Repair	$_____
Front Door	$_____
Front Storm Door	$_____
Rear Door	$_____
Rear Storm Door	$_____
Garage Door	$_____
Screened Porch	$_____
Patio	$_____
Front Stoop	$_____
Rear Stoop	$_____
Siding/Shingles Repair	$_____
Fascia Repair	$_____
Roof Repair	$_____
Other _____	$_____
Total	$_____

Interior

	Living Room	Dining Room
Floor Repair	$_____	$_____
Carpeting	$_____	$_____
Moldings	$_____	$_____
Walls	$_____	$_____
Closet Doors	$_____	$_____
Electrical Outlets	$_____	$_____
Electrical Fixtures	$_____	$_____
Air Conditioner	$_____	$_____
Heating Fixtures	$_____	$_____
Thermostat	$_____	$_____
Other _____	$_____	$_____
Other _____	$_____	$_____
Other _____	$_____	$_____
Total	$_____	$_____

Interior (Continued)

Kitchen		Bathroom	
Floor	$_____	Floor	$_____
Walls	$_____	Walls	$_____
Cabinets	$_____	Cabinets	$_____
Sink	$_____	Sink	$_____
Stove	$_____	Commode	$_____
Electrical Outlets	$_____	Electrical Outlets	$_____
Electrical Fixtures	$_____	Electrical Fixtures	$_____
Appliance Repair/ Replacement	$_____	Tub/Shower	$_____
Heating Fixtures	$_____	Heating Fixtures	$_____
Other _____	$_____	Other _____	$_____
Other _____	$_____	Other _____	$_____
Other _____	$_____	Other _____	$_____
Total	$_____	Total	$_____

Bedrooms

	Master Bedroom	Second Bedroom	Third Bedroom	Fourth Bedroom
Floors	$_____	$_____	$_____	$_____
Walls	$_____	$_____	$_____	$_____
Closet Doors	$_____	$_____	$_____	$_____
Moldings, Trim	$_____	$_____	$_____	$_____
Electrical Outlets	$_____	$_____	$_____	$_____
Electrical Fixtures	$_____	$_____	$_____	$_____
Air Conditioner	$_____	$_____	$_____	$_____
Heating Fixtures	$_____	$_____	$_____	$_____
Thermostat	$_____	$_____	$_____	$_____
Other _____	$_____	$_____	$_____	$_____
Other _____	$_____	$_____	$_____	$_____
Other _____	$_____	$_____	$_____	$_____
Total	$_____	$_____	$_____	$_____

Basement

	Estimated Cost
Stairs	$_____
Floor	$_____
Walls	$_____
Electrical Outlets	$_____
Electrical Fixtures	$_____
Heating Unit	$_____
Hot Water Unit	$_____
Air Conditioner	$_____
Plumbing Repairs	$_____
Water Lines	$_____
Oil Tank	$_____
Total	$_____

Painting

Exterior	$_____
Interior	$_____
Total	$_____
Overall Total Cost of Repair and Renovation	$_____

Overall Cost of Purchase

Bid Price $_____

Acquisition Costs $_____

Holding Costs $_____

Repairs and Renovations $_____

    Total $_____

Total Money Needed $_____

COST OF MONEY

$_____ @ _____% Interest $_____

Sales Costs $_____

Total Cost of Purchase and Sale $_____

   Ultimate Sale Price $_____

   Less Total Costs $_____

   Anticipated Profit $_____

Analysis

Sale Price in Renovated Condition $_____

Cost of Sale

Commission $_____

Legal Charge $_____

Stamps on Deed $_____

Preparation of Mortgage
Satisfaction $_____

Recording Satisfaction $_____

Title Closer Gratuity $_____

Total $_____

Holding Costs

Taxes - 6 months @ $_____

Insurance $_____

Utilities

  Oil $_____

  Gas $_____

  Electric $_____

  Water $_____

COST OF MONEY

$_____ @ _____% Interest $_____

6 months interest $_____

Acquisition Cost

Anticipated Bid Limit $_____

COST OF PURCHASE

Title Insurance $_____
Recorded Deed $_____

INDEX

ALSO AVAILABLE FROM ADAMS MEDIA:

The Everything® Money Book
by Rick Mintzer, with Kathi Mintzer

The *Everything® Money Book* is written simply to make handling, managing, saving, and possibly earning money easier. It provides suggestions so that anyone can achieve their financial goals: whether it's sending the kids to college, planning a superb vacation, or retiring in another state. The information is shared in easy-to-follow language, so even the first time budgeter won't be overwhelmed.

Trade paperback, $12.95
ISBN 1-58062-145-7

The Everything® Investing Book
by Rick Mintzer and Annette Racond

You can understand Wall Street, and make money investing with confidence in stocks, bonds, and mutual funds. This book starts at the very beginning with clear and simple explanations of your basic investment choices. You will learn which type of investment is best for you, and how to choose specific companies or mutual funds to invest in. You will also learn how to invest for specific goals, such as college education or retirement. With *The Everything® Investing Book*, you will learn how to build your wealth without taking unnecessary risks—and be able to clearly understand your investment choices.

Trade paperback, $14.95
ISBN 1-58062-149-X

Visit the entire Everything® series at everything.com

AVAILABLE WHEREVER BOOKS ARE SOLD

If you cannot find this title at your favorite retail outlet, you may order it directly from the publisher. BY PHONE: Call 1-800-872-5627. We accept Visa, MasterCard, and American Express. $4.95 will be added to your total order for shipping and handling. BY MAIL: Write out the full title of the book you'd like to order and send payment, including $4.95 for shipping and handling, to: Adams Media, 57 Littlefield Street, Avon, MA 02322. 30-day money-back guarantee.